GREAT MOMENTS
IN
AVIATION

This book was devised and produced by
Multimedia Books Ltd

Editor: Linda Osband
Design: Richard Carr:
            Strange Design Associates
Production: Zivia Desai

First published in the United States of America
in 1989 by Mallard Press

Mallard Press and its accompanying design and
logo are trade marks of BDD Promotional Book
Company, Inc.

ISBN 0-792-45039-6

Typeset by O'Reilly Clark, London
Origination by Imago Publishing Limited
Printed in Italy by Imago Publishing Limited

GREAT MOMENTS
— IN —
AVIATION

MICHAEL J H TAYLOR

MALLARD
PRESS

CONTENTS

Below
An early great moment in aviation came on 8 August 1709, when Father Bartolomeu de Gusmão became the first to demonstrate ascending flight with a model hot-air balloon. The balloon drifted to the window, causing the 'fire material' to ignite the paper envelope and then the curtains. (Air BP magazine)

INTRODUCTION

More than 300 years of demonstrated flight has witnessed many great moments in aviation, some glorious, others tragic, mingled and mixed with the humorous and the ridiculous. We may now laugh at Father Bartolomeu de Gusmão causing chaos in the ambassador's drawing-room at the Casa da India by accidentally setting fire to the curtains while showing off his model hot-air balloon to the court of King John V of Portugal, but it was a demonstration of huge historical importance. Fortunately 'His Majesty was good enough not to take ill'. Indeed, via the Montgolfier balloon experiments of the late 18th century, de Gusmão's 'burning' ambition has a direct historical link to the *Virgin Atlantic Flyer* that made the first transatlantic crossing by a hot-air balloon 277 years, 10 months and 25 days later, during 2-3 July 1987. Between these have been hundreds, maybe thousands, of great moments performed by courageous men and women in balloons, gliders, powered airplanes and spacecraft.

1

FIRST KNIGHT
OF THE AIR

History is full of stories of raw courage and daring. Little progress in flying could have been made without that special breed of men and women willing to risk their fortunes, reputations or lives in the pursuance of the science. Names such as Orville and Wilbur Wright, Louis Blériot, Charles Lindbergh and Neil Armstrong are emblazoned, yet these are few among the countless heroes and heroines of the air whose adventures have largely been forgotten to popular legend.

First Knight of the Air

Left
Model representation of the Montgolfier hot-air balloon which, on 21 November 1783, carried Francois Pilatre de Rozier and the Marquis d'Arlandes on the very first aerial journey. This epic ascent took place just 37 days after de Rozier became the first man ever to fly in a tethered balloon, on 15 October 1783. (United States Air Force Museum, Ohio).

Below
Richard Crosbie ascending from Ranelagh Gardens on 19 January 1785.

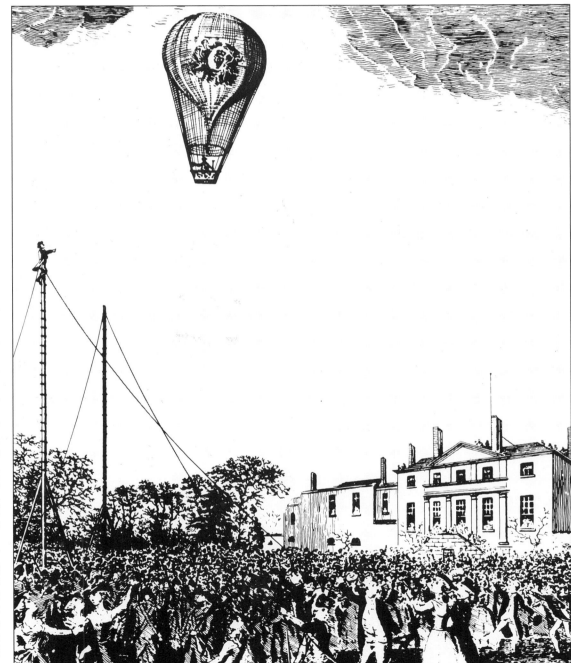

At the very dawn of flying, indeed only a mere 19 months after François Pilâtre de Rozier had become the very first man to fly in a tethered Montgolfier hot-air balloon, one such hero appeared. Then, having had his day, he quietly slipped away from memory. He was Richard McGwire, the first Knight of the air.

The setting was Ireland. The year 1784. The story began with Richard Crosbie, without whom McGwire would have remained pedestrian. Crosbie was a larger than life figure, well over 6 foot tall, overweight and good-hearted. From an aristocratic family, he had served with the Army but resigned his commission probably as the result of an inadequate independent income. Now he had new ambitions, not only to fly but to make money from it. What had inspired this highly unusual and dangerous venture is not certain, although on 15 April that year Mr Rosseau and a boy had flown from Dublin to Ratoath in an amazingly successful one-and-a-half hour balloon journey, an event Crosbie must have been at least aware of. Not a man to waste time, he set about trying to solve what was, in fact, an unsoluble problem, namely how to steer a balloon in flight and navigate it in a direction other than that dictated by the wind.

In a series of experiments he tested the effects of various surfaces in flowing water, successfully concluding that any control of a balloon would be at best marginal. As the gas balloon was a known entity, he concentrated his main efforts on the gondola. Light weight was essential, and the 'hull' of the boat-like gondola was constructed of linen or silk over a wooden frame. For power and control three systems were built into the design, comprising a large aft rudder, sails on two separate masts to which was also attached the cloth retaining the gas envelope, and two four-sail windmills that could be rotated by hand for manual propulsion. Named *Aeronautic Chariot*, it was exhibited at Ranelagh Gardens, Dublin, in August 1784. The *Aeronautic Chariot* probably never flew, but it is recorded that the hydrogen gas balloon from it was inflated and flew tethered on several occasions before finally being released carrying an animal passenger, Montgolfier fashion. It came down near the coast of the Isle of Man. What was to follow these successes needed to be spectacular. It was!

The final weeks of 1784 were spent on a new and larger balloon, which was completed in early January of the following year. With a conventional basket connected by ropes to the gas envelope, it made no pretence of artificial control. Crosbie put it on public exhibition at Ranelagh Gardens — the starting-point for his planned and perilous crossing of the Irish Sea that was to be attempted on the 10th — charging a shilling admission fee. As an early aviation entrepreneur, this gave him both publicity and cash. But bad weather forced postponement until the 19th.

On 19 January 1785 a crowd of 35-40,000 attended the lift-off. The advance publicity had done well and much money had changed hands. The assembled masses on the lawn of the stately home gave the event the atmosphere of a vast garden party, with the highly decorated balloon held between two high tethering poles forming the centerpiece. The Army attended to ensure control. A showman at heart, and like a prophet of the future, the smiling Crosbie boarded the balloon in the early afternoon. He had dressed for the occasion. Over a wrinkled waistcoat that ebbed and flowed around his large stomach and satin breeches stretched tight to his thighs, was carried a long oiled silk coat, lined and edged in fur. Fancy red boots came up to his calves, and on his wig sat an ornate leopard fur hat. He was, indeed, an aeronaut, for nobody else dressed like this!

But there was a serious side to Crosbie, and in the gondola were various apparatus for scientific use. To tumultuous cheering, the balloon was released and ascended skyward to the clouds. Within minutes it had passed from view. The wind took him in a northerly direction and through the gradually dimming daylight he could make out the coast approaching. Whether it had always been an intentioned possibility, or because of the wind direction, or even as it became clear that if he continued it

would be dark for the perilous sea crossing, he opened the gas valve and executed a controlled descent to alight at Clontarf. To see the rare sight of a man flying at all had thrilled the crowd, and Crosbie was carried as a hero to the residence of Lord Charlemont, one of the appointed organizers of the event.

By 12 May Crosbie had readied a second attempt, using the Palatine Square of the Dublin barracks as the starting-point. He was clearly confident of success, perhaps several times as sure, as each spectator had to part with five shillings to watch. At his signal the restraining ropes were released. To his horror the balloon refused to lift. Ballast and scientific apparatus were removed to lighten the load. Somewhat reluctantly the balloon ascended a little and began drifting towards houses, skimming their chimneys before thumping to the ground. The crowd became alarmed, but Crosbie was unhurt.

Not wanting to cancel the money-making event, perhaps even dreading the likely consequences, Crosbie (the entrepreneur) asked if there was a volunteer among the crowd of lighter weight than himself who would be willing to fly! Remarkably, there was. Out of the masses stepped Richard McGwire, a 21-year-old Trinity College undergraduate and army officer. Pushing his tricorne hat hard on to his head, he enthusiastically threw out

ballast and held tightly as the balloon ascended more easily and drifted north-easterly before turning with a westerly air stream. Eventually it crossed the coast and McGwire attempted to operate the gas release valve in order to descend. Nothing happened. He tried again. Nothing. Slowly the balloon drifted out to sea. In panic, he took the flag from the basket and tied a knife to the end of the pole. With bated breath he plunged it into the envelope. Gas escaped rapidly and the balloon lost height at an alarming but survivable rate. He came down into the sea some 9-10 miles out from Howth, but was thrown from the basket and into the chilling water. Fortunately, Lord Henry Fitzgerald had dispatched rescue sailing boats the moment he saw the balloon in trouble. Forty minutes later the exhausted McGwire was hauled from the water on the end of a gaff, his balloon still partially inflated and floating in the distance. A hero's reception awaited him in Dublin the next day, and he was received at the home of the Duke and Duchess of Rutland. To great popular approval the Lord Lieutenent bestowed a knighthood. Richard McGwire, the co-opted aeronaut and unsuspecting hero, had become the first Knight of the air. But where was Crosbie?

McGwire's epic, though short, flight had taken a good deal of the limelight from Crosbie, who now also had a challenger for the first Irish Sea flight in the form of a Frenchman, Potain. In the event, the pretender to the accolade also failed that June. But as if to add to Crosbie's problems, Dublin's Lord Mayor banned all further flights for reasons of public danger and absenteeism. Not to be beaten, Crosbie continued his preparations for 19 July, using the home of the Duke of Leinster as the rallying-point. The popular story says that Crosbie devised a ruse by which, if the flight was to go ahead, cannon would be fired two hours before take-off to allow spectators time to assemble on Leinster Lawn. This may indeed be so, but when the much depleted crowd did form after they heard cannon it included soldiers and a small military band! In fact, the morning weather was far from ideal for ballooning and the cannon call had been the work of an unknown hand or even an accident. But to cancel or fail yet again could well be the making of a riot. Inflating the balloon and preparing for the flight took several hours. Being summer, this time the light would hold good for the crossing. Yet, would there be a crossing? Still overweight, the balloon when released drifted and scraped the garden wall, descending and then flying up once more after 56 lb of ballast had been dropped. Once clear of obstacles, Crosbie waved a flag to the cheering people below.

The balloon ascended steadily, reaching such a high altitude that his barometer became redundant and his writing ink froze. He continued to drift out to sea above the worst weather. Presently, though, the high altitude cold began to tell on him. He also suffered sickness and an ear complaint. What is more, the balloon began moving off its easterly course. The gas valve was pulled to reduce height and hopefully pick up a more direct air current to the Welsh coast. This was a tragic mistake. The balloon descended into a violent storm. Nothing Crosbie did could prevent the inevitable, and bit by bit he lost height until at last the balloon struck the inhospitable water below. Bladders fitted to the basket kept it afloat, but the envelope became a great spinnaker, taking Crosbie further out to sea and away from the barge, *Captain Walmitt*, which was trying its best to catch the

runaway balloon and save its crew. In desperation Crosbie used a rope to extend the distance between the basket and the envelope, taking some of the wind out of the 'sail'.

On board ship, Crosbie began to recover. His cross-sea days were over, though he would fly once more, in 1786. While the ship's crew were dragging the balloon on deck high winds again caught the envelope, shooting it skyward like a vast kite on the end of a long rope and almost carrying a sailor with it! Plans to bring it on board were abandoned and the barge towed it along. Crosbie set foot on land at about 10.00 pm. A full 12 hours had passed since that unwanted cannon blast had set the flight in motion.

Crosbie received a hero's welcome on his return to Dublin. But for the storm he would almost certainly have managed the crossing, which would have been a fitting end to a journey he might, in truth, have believed beyond his capability earlier that year. So was he merely an entrepreneur, a gentle giant seeking fame and greater fortune, or a true pioneer in the accepted spirit of aviation? Probably both, and a man of great foresight and courage too. The same ambitions drove the Wright brothers more than a century later. But Crosbie's life was not to be long, and he died in 1800 at the age of 45.

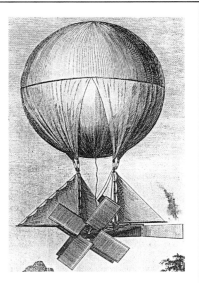

Above
Richard Crosbie's *Aeronautic Chariot*, put on exhibition in 1784.

Left
Richard Crosbie, Ireland's most celebrated early aeronaut (National Library of Ireland/Aer Lingus)

2

THE *FLYER* FLIES

'I see that Langley has had his fling and failed. It seems to be our turn to throw
now, and I wonder what our luck will be'.

Left
Wright *Flyer* of 17 December
1903, at the National Air and
Space Museum, Washington.

Below
Langley's full-sized *Aerodrome*
just before launching from its
houseboat on the Potomac river
in 1903. Twice it caught the
launcher on take-off and fell into
the river. It was the first airplane
capable of sustained flight. (US
Department of the Navy)

Bottom
Wright No. 1 glider of 1900, flown
as a kite. (Smithsonian Institution)

So wrote Wilbur Wright. American Professor Samuel Pierpont Langley had been experimenting with flight for longer than the Wright brothers. He had launched large powered models that had effortlessly flown over distances of up to 4,200 feet and yet still failed in his attempt to launch a full-size piloted airplane on 7 October 1903, even with a $50,000 US government state subsidy behind him. What chance of flight then had the self-supporting bicycle makers from Dayton, Ohio, sons of a bishop of the United Brethren in Christ church?

The extract from a letter gives a good insight to the Wright brothers, for Langley had been their greatest rival to the honor of achieving the world's first recognized manned and powered airplane flight. Yet the words from Wilbur indicate no panic, even though if Langley had succeeded the years of methodical work by the brothers would have been tainted at the eleventh hour. And they must have known Langley would try again, and soon. But they too were nearly ready.

Langley did make a second launching attempt, on 8 December 1903, which also failed. Orville had only learned of this as he returned by train to Kitty Hawk in North Carolina carrying new propeller shafts for the Wright airplane, the very time when he and his brother were preparing to make their bid for the skies. The newspaper carrying the story of Langley's failure was scathing, suggesting that he should have taken off 'bottom up', so that it would have gone up into the air and not down into the water. Were the Wrights any more sure of success? In truth, yes. Their careful experimentation had left little to chance, and if the immediate tests failed then they would learn from the mistakes and try again, just as they had in the past. It was only a matter of time before they would fly, and they knew it.

On the bitterly cold winter morning of 17 December 1903, the Wright brothers' newly built *Flyer* was taken from its shed and mounted on the launch trolley. Members from the Kill Devil Life Saving Station were to bear witness to the event. At 10.35 am Orville, lying on the bottom wing of the vibrant *Flyer*, gave the signal for release. The restraining wire was pulled and the airplane moved forward against a 27 mph headwind. Wilbur ran alongside the starboard wing, helping to steady the machine as it moved down the wooden rail. Then, suddenly, it rose and slowly headed away. For 12 glorious but breathtaking seconds Orville fought with the over-sensitive elevator, the undulating flight ending after just 120 feet when over-control caused the machine to dive to the ground. Just 12 seconds in the air! Far less time than they had managed in their gliders, yet it was the dawn of a new age. As for the demoralized Langley, the US government withdrew its support and he abandoned his flying experiments. Such was the price of success and failure.

For the Wrights this was just the beginning. That same day, after repairs to the *Flyer*, the brothers took turns to crew on three more occasions, their greater understanding of control allowing each to be of longer duration until the final flight covered 852 feet and lasted a magnificent 59 seconds. It was also the last flight of the *Flyer*, not only of the day but for good, as on landing the elevator was damaged. After being taken back to camp the *Flyer* was caught by strong winds, overturned and written off. It had served its purpose and had set speed, duration, altitude and distance records on its final flight that no other pioneering airplane could even approach for three long and unchallenged years.

Orville claimed for the *Flyer* three major achievements, namely having raised itself by its own power into the air, flown forward without reduction of speed, and landed safely at a point as high as that from which it had begun. At the time it was a good definition of the 'first flight', but as the work of earlier experimenting pioneers in America and Europe became better known and were recorded by historians, more adjectives were needed if the Wrights' event was not to be predated by the flights of others. The words 'sustained', 'controlled', 'powered' and 'heavier-than-air' machine had to be added, for if any was

omitted then someone else could claim to have flown first. And there were plenty of contenders. The steam-powered aircraft of Frenchman Felix du Temple 'hopped' into the air in 1874 after gathering speed down a ramp. Another steam aircraft was the work of Russian Alexander Fedorovich Mozhaiski in 1884, and Frenchman Clément Ader 'hopped' from level ground on 9 October 1890 in a steam-powered airplane of bat-like design. Even a 'hop' from water had been achieved by 1901, the Austrian Wilhelm Kress remembered also for adopting a petrol engine for his airplane. And there were others too, including the controversial Bavarian Gustav Whitehead, whose aviation achievements in America have never been officially recognized and have proven impossible for historians to substantiate.

The historic flights of 17 December were the culmination of four years of remarkable experimentation, development and trials. Four days later (the 21st), the industrialist Godfrey Cabot wrote to the Wrights enquiring if their machine could be used to transport tons of freight over a 16-mile route in West Virginia. The answer, of course, was no, and it was not until 7 November 1910 that a Wright biplane carried freight (the very first by air, comprising 542 yards of silk, at a cost of \$5,000 to the Morehouse-Martens Company of Columbus).

Orville and Wilbur Wrights' active interest in flying stemmed from the work of the German glider pioneer Otto Lilienthal, who had been killed while flying in 1896. Wilbur had been captivated by reports of Lilienthal's experiments and wondered if he could carry on his work, leading to a powered flying machine, just as Lilienthal himself had intended. More dynamic than his younger brother Orville, he quickly managed to share his enthusiasm, and the bicycle makers of Dayton, Ohio, began their historic course.

Four major hurdles confronted the brothers. The first was to gain practical experience of using gliders safely, so they 'could live long enough to learn to fly a powered machine'. The second problem was the necessity to devise a method of controlling their aircraft. The third hurdle was unexpected. From the wealth of

Above
Wright bicycle test rig used to compare the drag of a flat plate with that of aerofoil sections. (Smithsonian Institution)

Far Left
Wright No. 3 glider with its original twin fixed fins, being flown as a kite. (Smithsonian Institution)

Left
Wright No. 2 glider on the ground at Kill Devil Hills, with Wilbur showing the prone pilot's position. (Smithsonian Institution)

Right
Wilbur Wright at the controls of No. 3 glider. The twin fins had been replaced by a single rudder. In this configuration hundreds of controlled glides were made. (Smithsonian Institution)

published and available material, they thought the design of wings and aerofoil sections had been solved. It had not. The final major problem was one of power, the very 'brick wall' that had prevented the machines of early pioneers from flying well. They needed good output from a lightweight engine, which discounted steam.

Many earlier pilots had ignored the problem of control, and of those that did experiment, such as Lilienthal, a simple solution had been shifting the weight of their bodies to 'tilt' the aircraft in the direction required. This was practical for the gliders then being tested and a method still used today for hang-gliders, but of no value for large powered aircraft. In those early days 'weight shift' control required continual effort to achieve steady flight, a skill not attained by many pioneers.

An answer came after Wilbur Wright had spent some time watching birds. He recorded: 'My observations of the flight of buzzards leads me to believe that they regain their lateral balance when partly overturned by a gust of wind, by a torsion of the tips of the wings.' Later, this method became known as wing-warping.

After this important observation the brothers decided to build a model glider to test the practicality of wing-warping for lateral control. This was a biplane, with a wing span of just 5 feet. For test purposes the stagger of the wings could be varied and the horizontal stabilizer could be mounted in front or behind the wings. After flying the model as a kite, the Wrights considered that their idea for obtaining lateral and longitudinal control was along the right lines. Stage two was to set about designing a full-sized glider, this time one capable of carrying a man.

Completed in 1900, the biplane glider had a span of 17 feet and a wing and elevator area of 165 square feet. For such an important aircraft in the development of manned flight, it is remarkable that the glider cost just a few dollars to build. It weighed 52 lb. The pilot lay prone on the bottom wing in order to reduce drag, and the wings were warped by tightening a key wire

which, in turn, tightened other wires to twist (or warp) the ends of the wings. The aerodynamic effect was similar to that of present day ailerons. The elevator was located in front of the wings, as this was considered safer than behind in the event of a sudden nose-down attitude.

Typical of the Wrights' considered and logical approach to their experiments were their letters sent to elderly American glider designer Octave Chanute, asking for advice on suitable sites for flight testing, and to the Weather Bureau requesting wind information. It was on the advice of the Weather Bureau that the brothers chose Kitty Hawk. Not only were the winds strong and constant there, but the soft sand, they surmised, would lessen the impact of a crash! Of course, the Wrights owed much more to the generosity of Chanute, who gladly parted with technical information, including that on Pratt-trussed biplane structures.

Owing to its small size, the glider was flown mainly as an unmanned kite. For several tests the wings were rigged with some dihedral to provide automatic stability. In this form the glider flew badly in gusty conditions and the dihedral was abandoned. A few pilot-controlled kite flights were made as well as piloted free glides. The brothers were pleased with its performance and returned home to design Glider No. 2.

No. 2 had a bigger wing span of 22 feet and an area of 290 square feet. The wings had camber and an anhedral droop of 4 inches, and were warped by a foot-operated T-bar. It was taken to Kill Devil Hills, just south of Kitty Hawk, and tested in the summer of 1901. It did not fly well! To reduce the movement of the center of pressure the wing camber was reduced. In this form glides of up to 389 feet were made. More importantly, control was maintained in winds approaching 30 mph. But the lift developed was much less than it should have been according to tables published by Lilienthal. Most worrying of all was the tendency for the glider to nose up sharply and stall. But, on the plus side, the glider had proved immensely strong, having survived more than 40 landings. It was two despondent brothers who returned to Dayton, realizing that much of the published data they had accepted as fact was seriously in error.

To obtain the information sorely needed the brothers organized an amazing 10-month program of intensive research. It was this that gave them such a lead over all other pioneers and kept them years ahead. For this research they first used a simple bicycle rig, which allowed the 'lift' of different model wings to be measured as the bicycle was pedaled along. Although simple to fabricate, this rig was not a success. Instead they built a crude wind tunnel from a discarded starch box, with a fan providing the air flow. It was a huge success. Very quickly they discovered that the value taken by Lilienthal for the force on a flat plate perpendicular to the wind was only about 60 per cent of the actual value.

In a period of just two months the brothers tested more than 200 wing sections. They included monoplane, biplane and triplane arrangements. All the information obtained on air pressures, the aerodynamic properties of the aerofoils and the control surfaces was carefully recorded. The extent and accuracy of the experiments far exceeded that of any previous pioneers.

The applied result of all this information was Glider No. 3, built during August and September 1902. This had a span of 32 feet and a wing area of 305 square feet, with a slender varying camber. The wing-warping system was similar to that of the 1901 glider, but was operated by the pilot's hips sliding sideways on a wooden cradle. The elevator was still in front of the wings, but a major change was the addition of two fixed vertical fins.

The new glider was tested at Kill Devil Hills during September and October. It flew well in some glides, but when the wings were warped to regain level flight the aircraft began to spin. The brothers realized that the problem lay in what is known today as aileron drag. The twin rudders also caused problems. In side slips the fins tended to rotate the wings about their vertical axis. This problem was overcome by replacing the two fixed fins with a single steerable rudder with, importantly, the control cables attached to the wing-warping cradle. This vital step enabled the rudder to more than compensate for the warp-drag and resulted in an aircraft able to make smooth, banked turns.

With the glider in this configuration, the brothers made hundreds of controlled glides, achieving a maximum distance of 622 feet and a duration of 26 seconds. Now it was two satisfied brothers that returned home that winter.

With this experience behind them the brothers knew they needed only one more ingredient to make a powered airplane: a petrol engine! No suitable power plant was available, so the problem was overcome by designing and building their own in just six weeks. It produced 12 hp for a weight of 170 lb. They also designed and constructed two very efficient propellers, driven

from the engine by bicycle chains.

A new flying machine was designed to complement the engine. Known as the *Flyer*, it was again a biplane, with a 40 foot span and 510 square foot area. It weighed 605 lb without the pilot. The engine was mounted off-center on the lower wing, and to compensate for its weight the starboard side of the wing was built 4 inches longer than the port to provide additional lift.

The *Flyer* was taken to the now familiar Kill Devil Hills in September 1903, where the Wrights had left Glider No. 3. They were dismayed at finding the camp in disarray and the glider damaged. Lesser men might have rushed headlong into an early attempt at powered flight, but the Wrights always put safety first. The glider was repaired so that they could reacquaint themselves with the air before attempting a powered flight. During October they made only gliding flights, including one of 43 seconds on the 4th. But now the time had come. How frustrating it must have been when, on the first occasion of starting up the *Flyer's* engine, it backfired and bent a propeller shaft. New shafts arrived at Kitty Hawk on 20 November, but these also were too weak. As before, the job needed the Wrights' own touch and Orville returned to Dayton to make them himself. The aircraft was again ready for flight on 14 December, six days after Professor Langley had made his second and last attempt to launch his own *Aerodrome*.

It was the flick of a coin that was to decide which of the Wright brothers was to make the world's first airplane flight. Wilbur won. With the engine running smoothly, the *Flyer* took off from

Right
The historic first flight of a manned, powered and controlled airplane, with Orville as pilot.

its bicycle hub trolley after a downhill run of about 40 feet along the launching rail. Wilbur attempted to gain height too rapidly and stalled, causing the aircraft to plough back on the sand after just three-and-a-half seconds. It was a 'hop', not a flight. It was, therefore, Orville that took the controls for the next attempt, which had to be the following Thursday (17th) to gain the right weather conditions. The wind was strong enough for the take-off to be attempted from level ground. The rest is history.

To the *Flyer* can be accorded yet one more 'first'. On its historic flights it carried the first flight data recorders, in the form of a counter for engine revolutions, an air gauge to measure the distance flown, and a watch to determine flight duration.

The story of the first recognized flight of a manned and powered airplane ended there. The Wrights went back to Dayton and designed improved aircraft based on the same general layout. The new *Flyer II* covered a remarkable two-and-three-quarter miles on 9 November 1904, and on 5 October 1905 Wilbur piloted the *Flyer III* on an historic 24-mile journey. Elsewhere in America and Europe another year was to pass before anyone else could claim 'sustained' flight at all, then only lasting seconds!

Having proven their overwhelming superiority, remarkably the Wrights gave up flying completely in order to promote their airplane internationally. Wilbur had written to his father in September 1903, '. . . I think there is a slight possibility of achieving fame and fortune from it.' With the same coolness that had greeted Langley's contention to be the first to fly, so they set about the business of making money and defending their patents. The latter eventually led to an ironic twist of history. By way of fighting an injunction the Wright brothers had filed against them, the Curtiss company attempted to challenge the Wrights' 'first' claims. A bizarre attempt (of several) was the restoration of Langley's *Aerodrome*. Given new pontoons by Curtiss, it was flown at Hammondsport on 28 May 1914. The *Aerodrome* had indeed proven to be the 'first man-carrying machine capable of flight', as claimed by the Smithsonian Institution.

Meanwhile, the Wright brothers had not begun flying again until 6 May 1908, a three-year period during which they had lost most of their technical lead, allowing others to catch up and then overtake them. But the effect was not immediate, and on 2 August 1909 the Wrights sold the very first military airplane to the US Army. This aircraft, named *Miss Columbia*, cost the Army a cool $30,000, a price that included a bonus for exceeding the speed specifications. It was while Orville had been demonstrating a Wright biplane to the Army at Fort Myer in September of the previous year that he had crashed to the ground from a height of about 75 feet, an accident that killed his passenger Lieutenant Thomas Etholen Selfridge of the Signal Corps. Selfridge was the very first airplane fatality. Orville had miraculously escaped serious injury, but it was an accident he never really got over.

History also records that it was from Wright biplanes of later type that the first explosive bombs were dropped (7 January 1911) and the first machine-gun fired (2 June 1912). Yet the Wrights had been saddened to see the airplane as a machine of war. Orville said in 1917, 'When my brother and I built and flew the first man-carrying flying machine, we thought that we were

introducing into the world an invention which would make further wars practically impossible. What a dream it was; what a nightmare it has become.' Orville was alone to see the destructive use of the airplane, for his elder brother, Wilbur, had died on 30 May 1912 from typhoid fever. Among the very last Wright airplanes proper was the Model K seaplane, going to the US Navy in 1914. It still used chain drive and wing-warping! In 1915 Orville sold his rights in the Wright Aeronautical Company. It was the end of the line. Orville lived on until 1948, into the jet age.

Above
Only Orville survived the crash of the Wright military airplane, 17 September 1908. (US Air Force)

Below
Wright military airplane during trials at Fort Myer, Virginia, September 1908. (US Air Force)

3

A MOST IMPORTANT LANDING

14 November 1910. The day had been heavy with rain. Near the top of a sloping 83 foot long and 24 foot wide wooden platform constructed hastily only the day before over the bow of the US Navy's new light cruiser, USS *Birmingham*, stood the Curtiss *Hudson Flier* biplane. Already a famous aircraft, having picked up in May the New York *World* newspaper prize of $10,000 for a flight between Albany and New York, on it now hung the pride of the US Navy.

Left
Ely's biplane after landing on USS *Pennsylvania*. Note the dragged sandbags used to arrest the aircraft after touchdown. (US Department of the Navy)

Below
Eugene Ely at the controls of the *Hudson Flier,* with Glenn Curtiss looking on. (US Department of the Navy)

Hoisted on board the cruiser by crane that morning, the *Hudson Flier* was intended to make history, to be the first airplane to fly off a ship. It was not owned by the Navy, nor did the Navy have any other airplanes. At its controls was Eugene Ely, a co-opted civilian pilot working for the newly established Curtiss Exhibition Company.

Official US Navy interest in boat-launched airplanes had originated in 1898. On 25 March that year Theodore Roosevelt, then Assistant Secretary of the Navy, suggested that naval officers should be part of a board established to assess the military potential of model (and later full-size) airplanes being launched experimentally from a houseboat on the Potomac river by elderly mathematician and physicist Professor Samuel Pierpont Langley. Since 1896 Langley had flown his steam-powered model *Aerodromes* over long distances, but the culminating full-sized airplane of 1903 fouled its houseboat launcher on take-off in October and again in December, falling into the river and thereby allowing the Wright brothers to take the 'first flight' honors. The Wrights themselves went on to build the first military airplane for the US Army; two Navy observers had been present at Fort Myer in September 1908 during military demonstrations of the Wright biplane. This, however, did nothing to encourage the Secretary of the Navy to purchase a similar airplane at the time.

Incredibly, it was the innovation of a newspaper that heralded the great about-turn that eventually brought the Navy into aviation. On 19 January 1910 Lieutenant Paul Beck had dropped sandbags over Los Angeles from an airplane piloted by Louis Paulhan. Clearly, ships too would be as vulnerable to air attack. The *World* newspaper was convinced airpower held the key to future battles, and to press the point it sponsored an effective demonstration that June. Flagged buoys in the shape of a battleship were set out on Lake Keuka. On the 30th Glenn Curtiss, anxious for any opportunity to promote his airplanes and fledgling company, flew a mock attack at a height of 50 feet with pieces of lead pipe falling as dummy bombs.

The point of the exercise had been well made. On 26 September 1910 Captain Washington Irving Chambers was appointed officer in charge of assessing progress in aviation from a naval viewpoint. At last matters were moving in the right direction, albeit cautiously. That October Chambers was assigned two assistants, one of whom was Naval Constructor William McEntee who had been at the Fort Myer demonstrations of 1908. An immediate job for the small team was to investigate the difficulties associated with providing room for airplanes or airships on board future scouting ships, as recommended to the Secretary of the Navy by the General Board on 1 October. Yet, despite promising moves, the Secretary took no firm steps to actually purchase an airplane, although two such requests were made that month by the Bureau of Construction and Repair. Indeed, so anxious was the Bureau to obtain an airplane for the Navy, it went as far as to suggest that the builders of the forthcoming battleship, USS *Texas*, should be instructed to include one or more as part of the modified design specifications.

As luck would have it, the final push into aviation came from an entirely unexpected quarter, again the *World* newspaper inadvertently forcing the pace. In concert with the Hamburg-American Steamship Line, the aviation-minded newspaper announced plans to fly an airplane from an ocean liner to speed mail in an experimental and pioneering service. A fascinating and progressive concept, years before its time, it could also have unknowingly benefited the Imperial German Navy. Pilot for the experiment was to be the Canadian James A. D. McCurdy, who had himself been closely associated with Glenn Curtiss's earliest

airplanes. Flying the Curtiss No. 4, McCurdy had made the first airplane flight in Canada on 23 February 1909, and on 27 August 1910 he had sent and received the first radio messages between an airplane and the ground while flying a Curtiss over Sheepshead Bay, New York State.

Chambers and his team had also been considering a similar experiment, and news of the competition stirred hurried efforts to be first. But the Steamship Line was far advanced. The 5th of November 1910 was scheduled to be the date for the civil fly-off. Fortunately for the Navy, at the last moment the attempt had to be put back. The race was on again. But Chambers needed a ship, fast! On the 9th the Navy assigned USS *Birmingham* to the experiment. Chambers now had a ship, but no airplane. No doubt at McEntee's recommendation, he raced to where Wilbur Wright was taking part in an aviation event, but was too late to meet him face to face. A quick telephone conversation dashed any hope of cooperation. Then, quite by chance, Chambers met up with Ely, who immediately volunteered his services. It was the

Below
Ely makes the historic first take-off from a ship, 14 November 1910. Behind USS *Birmingham* is USS *Roe*, used for plane guard. (US Department of the Navy)

kind of enterprise he specialized in, although entirely different from anything he had attempted so far in his year and a half as a pilot. The 19th of November was to be the big day.

But competition worked both ways, and not to be out-done the Hamburg-American Steamship Line's *Pennsylvania* was substituted for the planned *Amerika* liner to bring forward its fly-off. All was made ready for the 12th, for the *World* newspaper knew there was little news value in being second. The Navy was to be beaten after all.

In a final and fateful flight check prior to weighing anchor, the engine of McCurdy's airplane was started on board ship. By chance a can had been left too close and the spun propeller struck it. The damage was serious. The take-off would have to be postponed again until a replacement propeller was secured. This was a stroke of fortune Chambers could not miss. USS *Birmingham* was readied the next day by feverish work.

On the 14th, poor weather conditions twice delayed USS *Birmingham* sailing from Hampton Roads, Virginia. By early afternoon the skies began to clear and it prepared to sail. The plan was for Ely to take advantage of headwinds as the ship steamed at 20 knots. But with so much delay Ely became impatient. The engine of his airplane was started before the ship moved. It nearly cost him the flight!

With the ship still at rest, Ely gave the signal for release and at 3.16 pm the 'stick and string' biplane began to gather speed down the platform. Without sufficient headwind or forward speed to gain enough lift, the biplane left the end of the platform and made a frightening but steady descent to the water. The crew on board the ship lost sight of it. Ely struggled with the stick, but the airplane glanced the water. Moments later it reappeared, slowly

Left
Having eaten, Ely took off again from the cleared deck of USS *Pennsylvania* on 18 January 1911. (US Department of the Navy)

Below Left
Ely approaches USS *Pennsylvania* on 18 January 1911, sailors taking every vantage-point to witness the event. (US Department of the Navy)

Right
Lieutenant Theodore G. Ellyson, the first US Navy aviator. (US Department of the Navy)

Below Right
Curtiss A-1 *Triad* hydro aeroplane, the US Navy's first airplane. (US National Archives)

climbing and heading out to joyous applause. Originally intending to fly to the Norfolk Navy Yard, Ely instead headed for the nearest land and came down on Willoughby Spit, a little over two miles distant. After landing he appreciated quite how lucky he had been. His brush with the water had damaged both blades of the propeller!

Chambers and Ely had won for the Navy more than merely a place in history. They had demonstrated a means by which scouting ships could extend their 'eyes' over the horizon. But now it was the turn of Chambers to show caution. Amid a flurry of suggestions on how the Navy could quickly adapt its ships to carry airplanes, he decided that a further 'landing on' experiment was needed to assess the airplane's full potential.

Although Ely was to perform the 'landing', on 29 November Glenn Curtiss offered to train a Navy officer to fly free of charge. This was accepted, and on 23 December Lieutenant Theodore

Above
Glenn Curtiss and his hydro-
aeroplane being hoisted on board
USS *Pennsylvania* on 17 February
1911. (US Department of the
Navy)

G. Ellyson was sent to the Glenn Curtiss Aviation Camp at North Island, San Diego. Here, in addition to flight training, he helped Curtiss make preparations for what were to be the very first premeditated landing, taxi and take-offs in a hydroaeroplane (seaplane), when on 26 January 1911 Curtiss took off from the harbor, alighted, taxied around, took off again, flew about a mile and alighted once more. Another milestone for future naval operations had been reached. The importance of this early trial became apparent on 17 February, when Curtiss taxied to the anchored *Pennsylvania*, was lifted on board by crane, and was subsequently lowered back to the water, where he took off.

Meanwhile, little time had been wasted in preparing for the landing experiment, and a 119 foot 4 inch long and 31 foot 6 inch wide sloping wooden platform was constructed over the stern of the cruiser USS *Pennsylvania*. At Ellyson's suggestion, an aircraft arresting system was devised. Two 12 inch high and well-

spaced rails ran the length of the platform, across which were stretched 22 ropes, each about 3 feet apart. At the ends of each rope were tied 50 lb sandbags, lying on the platform but free to be dragged along. To the new Curtiss Model D-IV biplane (in fact, a similar machine in most respects to the *Hudson Flier* but most noticeably having extra wing panels between the outer sections of the wings) were attached six hooks, intended to snatch the ropes and slow the airplane's forward speed. As final safety measures, a canvas screen was erected to protect the ship's superstructure against collision, and Ely donned the usual light sporting leather helmet, goggles and a partially inflated inner tube for buoyancy if he ditched; similar equipment was to be requested by Ellyson in September 1911, as the first official Navy request for flight clothing.

Flying from Selfridge Field, San Francisco, on the morning of 18 January 1911, Ely circled the cruiser and then made his

approach to the anchored ship in San Francisco Bay. He had to allow for a difficult tailwind. At a fraction past 11.00 am he flew over the stern and switched off engine power. The airplane came down and caught the 12th and subsequent ropes, pulling the sandbags inwards and stopping in only 30 feet. It was a complete triumph. The ship's captain, C. F. Pond, reputedly remarked, 'This is the most important landing of a bird since the dove flew back to the Ark.' But the day was not over. After an early and quick lunch (while the crew cleared the platform of the ropes and sandbags), at 11.58 Ely took off from the *Pennsylvania* and flew back to Selfridge Field. The aircraft carrier had arrived! But perhaps fate demanded a price to be exacted. On 14 October 1911 Ely was killed in an unrelated flying accident. For all his momentous achievements on behalf of the Navy he had been given only a single small cash award, by the US Aeronautical Reserve. A quarter of a century was to pass before Ely was to receive (posthumously) just and meaningful reward, the Distinguished Flying Cross for outstanding contributions to marine aviation.

On 4 March 1911 the US Congress provided the Bureau of Navigation with the sum of $25,000 for experimental aviation work. This was used in part to fund two Curtiss and a Wright aircraft. The first of these, a Curtiss A-1 *Triad*, made its first four flights in the early evening of 1 July 1911, twice with Ellyson at the controls. On the 3rd, again flying from Lake Keuka, Ellyson became the first naval pilot to undertake a night flight. The A-1 was also Ellyson's mount on 31 July 1912, when the first attempt was made to catapult the airplane using compressed air. Although the experiment ended with the A-1 and its pilot dumped in the water, Ellyson was successfully catapult-launched in the Curtiss A-3 (another of the Navy Type I series aircraft that began with A-1) at Washington Navy Yard on 12 November that same year. Another progressive step had been achieved.

In another much later experiment, following the catapult-launch of Curtiss flying-boat AB-2 from an anchored barge on 16 April 1915, AB-2 became the first airplane to be catapulted from a warship, on 5 November, launched from the stern of USS *North Carolina*. Interestingly, as C-2 (AB-2's designation prior to the

Above Left
Commander Charles Rumney Samson, Royal Navy, flew the first airplane off a moving ship, on 9 May 1912. Here his Short S.38 rises from HMS *Hibernia*. (Shorts)

Left
The C-2 flying-boat catapult launched from USS *North Carolina*. (US Department of the Navy)

Right
Squadron Commander Dunning successfully lands his Sopwith Pup on HMS *Furious*, deck crew rushing forward to stop the fighter by grabbing hanging straps. The next attempt cost him his life.

Type Cs becoming ABs in March 1914) it had earlier demonstrated the use of a Sperry gyroscopic automatic pilot, on 30 August 1913. Trial flights with AB flying-boats from *North Carolina* continued until 12 July 1916, when AB-3 was launched while the ship was steaming. This battleship gained the honor of becoming the first vessel in the US Navy designated to carry and launch aircraft.

By then, however, more than two years had passed since US Navy pilots had gone to war. On 20-21 April 1914, five AH hydroaeroplanes and AB flying-boats had sailed from Pensacola for Vera Cruz on board USS *Birmingham* and *Mississippi* during the Mexican crisis. Lieutenant P. N. L. Bellinger is recorded as having flown the first mission in AB-3 on the 25th, and while flying AH-3 on 6 May he sustained the first war damage to a Navy aircraft (rifle fire).

With the commissioning of USS *Langley* on 20 March 1922, the Chambers/Ely dream of the American aircraft carrier proper came to fulfilment. But, meanwhile, war against Germany had given Britain the earlier resolve to put the world's first aircraft carriers proper into operational service, beginning with HMS *Furious*. This had its price, and Britain too had suffered the consequences of innovation. While as early as 9 May 1912 Commander Charles Rumney Samson had flown from the battleship HMS *Hibernia* to record the world's first take-off from a moving ship, it was not until 2 August 1917 that Britain's Squadron Commander E. H. Dunning made the very first flight on to a moving ship, side-slipping his Sopwith Pup fighter on to the forecastle deck of *Furious*. During a second attempt on the 7th, Dunning was carried over the bow and killed. The aircraft carrier as we know it today was, indeed, hard won!

4

WARNEFORD VC

'Zeppelin, help us in war. England will be burned out!' The chant rang through the German people. The Zeppelin airships had the power.

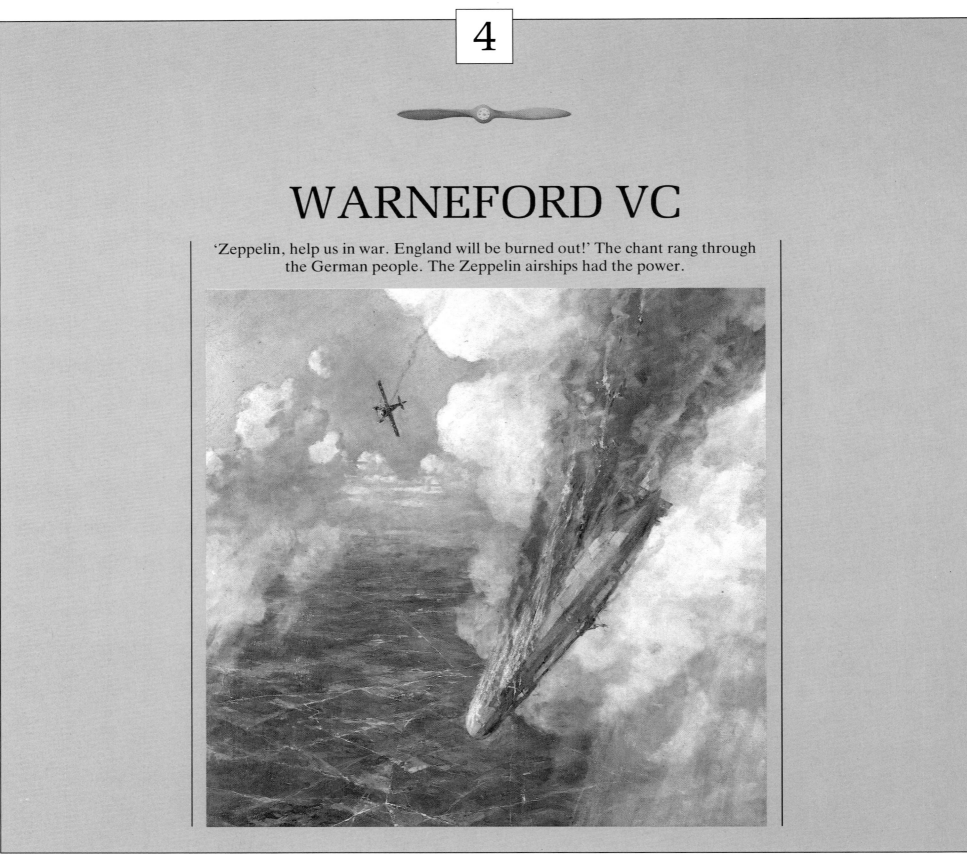

Below
This rare photograph is the only one known to show Zeppelins in formation during an operational mission. Here Naval Airship Division L13 nearest, L11 and L12 to rear (LZ 45, LZ 41 and LZ 43) fly with L9 and L10 (LZ 36 and LZ 40) on a five-ship raid against England, 9-10 August 1915. L12 was hit by gunfire over England and went down. (Imperial War Museum)

Left
Lieutenant Warneford's Great Exploit by Gordon Crosby. (Imperial War Museum)

To the consternation of Germany, Britain had not remained for long on the side-lines watching the most powerful and best-equipped army in the world march to subjugate Russia and France, taking little Luxembourg and Belgium in its path. Germany's Schlieffen Plan for the conquest of its enemies dated from 1905, and it had cloaked its 1914 mobilization by claiming to be taking merely a precautionary response to Russia's own mobilization after Austria-Hungary threatened Serbia. Germany might have believed it was fulfilling its destiny in Europe, but on 4 August 1914 the British Empire stood by passively no longer. War was declared! The German people were stunned and angered. But how to strike at England? The Royal Navy ruled the seas. 'Zeppelins fly to England, you dark and silent raiders.'

The Great War, the first of the World Wars as it turned out, the War to End Wars if one was an optimist in 1914-18, started much as those of earlier times. Great land armies attacked in lines and waves, advanced further, then retreated to count the dead, only now on a bigger stage and in greater numbers. Cavalry still sped with swords glinting and guns blazing, and the countryside turned from autumn to winter without the seasons changing, the leafless trees like islands in swamps of mud.

Only, was it the same? Soon the cavalry had gone, some of its number later mounting airplanes not horses. Rittmeister (Cavalry Captain) Manfred von Richthofen had been one, transferred from the Eastern Front to the German Air Service in May 1915, and earning the name 'Red Baron' for shooting down 80 Allied aircraft before he too died in the cockpit. The airplane and airship had changed warfare, and quickly their ability to reconnoitre from the air made them indispensable to those on the ground.

But aircraft were not just airborne 'eyes'. They could be offensive weapons too. From the outbreak of hostilities the British War Office believed Germany would use its airships to bomb Britain. At this early stage in aerial warfare airships alone were capable of making flights of long duration while carrying a useful bombload. For the first time the mighty Royal Navy, the world's greatest sea power, appeared incapable of defending Britain's shores and its subjects from attack by enemies across the seas.

Not so, was the cry! The British War Office *was* overstretched in its capacity to supervise war efforts both at home and abroad, but the Admiralty was not. On 1 July 1914 the Royal Naval Air Service had come into being, formed out of the Naval Wing of the Royal Flying Corps. By August 1914 it had 71 airplanes, 7 airships and a personnel of over 800. The Admiralty was ideally suited to take over the task of home defense, and this it did on 3

September 1914.

Right at the start the Admiralty had two cards up its sleeve. The first was that its pre-war bombing experiments had enabled it to stockpile a useful supply of bombs, including the 20 lb Hales type that detonated on impact; the second that its Eastchurch Squadron had been stationed at Dunkirk in France since 1 September. Here, then, was an opportunity not only to defend against the air menace but to destroy it on the ground.

Arming aircraft had not been taken too seriously pre-war, and the Squadron's only permanently armed aircraft at the time was the Astra-Torres airship No. 3, which had just been returned to England. On the 22nd, flying from Antwerp, four RNAS airplanes set out to attempt the first air raid on Germany, armed with Hales bombs. Airship sheds at Cologne and Düsseldorf were the targets, two airplanes intending to attack each. In the event only Flight Lieutenant Collet in his Avro 504 found his target, and none of the three bombs dropped exploded. All airplanes and crews returned safely. On 8 October two of Eastchurch Squadron's Sopwith Tabloids set out to raid the same sheds. Mist prevented Squadron Commander Spenser-Grey locating the Cologne sheds so he dropped his bombs on the railway station instead. But Flight Lieutenant Marix bombed a Düsseldorf shed from an altitude of about 600 feet and destroyed Zeppelin LZ 25 (Z.IX) that was housed inside. The resulting flames shot hundreds of feet into the air. But flying so low had its dangers, and Marix's aircraft was hit by gunfire. He eventually returned to base on a borrowed bicycle. This was the first successful air attack on Germany.

So the raids went on. But it was not to be one-sided. On 19 January 1915 the German Navy opened its account against Britain by sending out three Zeppelins (L3, L4, and L6) from Fuhlsbüttel and Nordholz. L6 returned early with engine problems, but the other two struck at Great Yarmouth, Sheringham, Thornham, Brancaster, Hunstanton, Heacham, Snettisham and King's Lynn, the high-explosive and incendiary bombs leaving 4 dead and 15 injured. Zeppelin raids against London began on the night of 31 May-1 June 1915, when LZ 38 dropped 3,000 lb of bombs. Seven Britons were killed and 14 injured.

So the cat and mouse went on. German Zeppelin and Schütte-Lanz rigid airships were used by both the Navy and Army, although the Naval Airship Division operated the largest number (69 by the war's end). History records that the Division lost a massive 40 percent of its total personnel, greater than any other branch of the German fighting services, but back in early 1915 it seemed almost charmed. Bristling with machine-guns, extremely high flying and almost silent, little could touch its airships, and what damage they took during operations could mostly be absorbed. Anti-aircraft batteries aided by searchlights (when there were some) had marginal success, but Allied airplanes had difficulty flying high enough to intercept and, anyway, were insufficiently armed. Notable exceptions, though, had been on the night of 17-18 May, when LZ 38 had been intercepted at a low 2,000 feet by Flight Sub-Lieutenant Mulock flying an Avro 504, but his gun had jammed, while sister Army airship LZ 39 had taken damage from RNAS airplanes while at about 10,000 feet over Belgium.

One of the pilots attacking LZ 39 had been Flight Sub-Lieutenant R. A. J. Warneford. He was a pilot with No. 1 Squadron, RNAS, a unit that had been ordered overseas in February 1915 to relieve Wing Commander Charles Samson's Eastchurch Squadron. On this occasion the airship had climbed away from him. Significant during the 17-18 May interceptions had been the British use of new incendiary bullets, designed not only to pierce the many bags in an airship's envelope but to ignite the hydrogen gas itself. Clearly the bullets had not worked properly. New types of explosive ammunition were invented.

On the night of 6-7 June 1915 the same three Army Zeppelins were sent out to raid London. Hauptmann Erich Linnarz commanding LZ 38 very quickly had to give up the mission as his airship developed engine problems. Mist or fog covered the sea, making the raid on England difficult, and so it was decided that

Flight Sub-Lieutenant R. A. J. Warneford VC. (Imperial War Museum)

the two remaining airships would divert for their secondary target, the railway complex at Calais.

Meanwhile, in the very early hours of the 7th, Warneford had set out to bomb the Zeppelin sheds at Berchem St Agathe. However, at Ostend he saw an airship. It was the Zeppelin LZ 37 commanded by Oberleutnant van der Haegen. Warneford trailed it to Ghent, kept at a distance by fierce machine-gun fire from the airship's gunners. But he was not going to lose another Zeppelin. The airship climbed. Warneford did his best to follow, the tiny 80 hp Le Rhone engine of his French Morane-Saulnier Type L *3253* straining. His airplane could climb at only some 340 feet per minute at best. None the less, he reached a magnificent 11,000 feet, at which he was some 150 feet above the airship. The fury of the machine-gunners made only a single pass possible. He dived for the target, dropping out six Hales bombs as he passed over. The last exploded, sending LZ 37 crashing down in flames. The wreck fell on a convent in the suburbs of Ghent, killing two nuns. Only one member of LZ 37's crew survived.

Warneford had been caught by the blast from the exploding Zeppelin, sending his airplane into a spin. He gained control and made a forced landing behind enemy lines to mend a broken fuel line, 35 minutes later setting off triumphantly to base. LZ 37 had

been the first airship destroyed by an air attack. The following evening Warneford was told he had been awarded the Victoria Cross, Britain's highest military honor. He also received the Chevalier of the Legion of Honour.

It was the beginning of the end for the German airship bombers, and seemed to demoralize the Army and Naval Airship Division crews. The crews, already strained on the long missions to Britain, soon faced more confident anti-aircraft guns and better armed airplanes, their presence illuminated by searchlights and phosphor shells.

Meanwhile, LZ 39 commanded by Hauptmann Masius had again evaded destruction, taking cover in cloud while under airplane attack. LZ 38 was less lucky. Flying Henry Farman biplanes from Dunkirk in the darkness of the same morning (the 7th), RNAS pilots Flight Lieutenant Wilson and Flight Lieutenant Mills found the airship in its shed at Evere. While preparing to attack they were illuminated by searchlights. By deception they escaped the anti-aircraft guns and released 15 bombs on target, causing a massive fire and total destruction.

Warneford, though, had little time to enjoy the fame he had earned. While flying a similar Henry Farman biplane near Paris 10 days later, the tail collapsed in mid-air and he was killed.

Morane-Saulnier Type L parasol monoplane *3253*, one of 25 used by the RNAS and Flight Sub-Lieutenant Warneford's mount for the famous attack on Zeppelin LZ37. (Imperial War Museum)

5

RACING THE WAVES

Just six years after the Wright brothers had first coaxed their *Flyer* into the air, Reims in France hosted the world's first international aviation competition meeting (August 1909). But, while conventional airplanes were then still few, water-borne seaplanes were very rare indeed.

Left
Britain's Sopwith Schneider
winning the 1914 trophy event,
as depicted in this painting by
Mr Kenneth McDonough. (Royal
Air Force Museum, Hendon)

Below
La Coupe d'Aviation Maritime
Jacques Schneider — the
Schneider Trophy.

To help remedy this, in late 1912 a French aviation and motoring enthusiast by the name of Jacques Schneider, son of a wealthy armaments manufacturer, offered *La Coupe d'Aviation Maritime Jacques Schneider* (better known merely as the Schneider Trophy) and a cash prize of £1,000 (for each of three consecutive years) to the winner of a hydroaeroplane contest. In the knowledge that some 70 percent of the Earth's surface is covered by water, Schneider was not alone in believing that the development of reliable seaplanes able to operate to and from water would speed international communications. Therefore, the rules for the contest included seaworthiness tests for the competing aircraft and a race of at least 150 nautical miles. Speed was regarded as paramount, for Schneider knew that in the world of motor sport the quest for speed had developed both endurance and reliability. But as the following paragraphs will relate, the Schneider Trophy contest did not so much help speed international communications as achieve that other goal, to stimulate airframe and engine development. Indeed, it is not overstating the point to say that from Reginald J. Mitchell's involvement with the Supermarine entries in the Schneider Trophy was born much of the know-how that allowed him to progress on to the famous Spitfire fighter that helped the Royal Air Force in perilous times.

The first contest, a little-noted item in the Monaco Hydro-Aeroplane Meeting of April 1913, gained only minor attention. Maurice Prévous of France was the winner, despite the performance of his Deperdussin monoplane being penalized by a 'birdcage' of bracing wires. However, there was general agreement that this small and almost overlooked event had been the most successful, causing a great deal of excitement. Designers and manufacturers began to look ahead to 1914, and it was soon seen that Schneider's contest had created huge international interest, with entries from the USA, Britain, France, Germany and Switzerland. As in the previous year, the 1914 meeting was at Monaco. From the outset there was a hubbub of anticipation about this second Schneider contest, with a total of 12 entries from the five nations.

Britain's Tommy Sopwith, who in 1913 had established the Sopwith Aviation Company at Kingston-upon-Thames, Surrey, decided that if he could carry off the Schneider Cup in 1914 it would gain valuable publicity for his new venture. The company's Tabloid biplane was chosen for development as the Sopwith Schneider, requiring a more powerful engine and water-borne capability. The latter was provided by one ungainly wide-span float which almost caused disaster, cartwheeling the aircraft into the Thames when tested just 16 days before the contest. Near panic ensued to salvage and prepare the Schneider within the two weeks remaining, and resulted in the single float being sliced in half to make two floats. After a second Thames test showed that stability had been gained, the aircraft was shipped to Monaco. There bad weather at first delayed essential flight testing. But this delay also helped Sopwith by giving time for improvements.

The 1914 event began as a 'piece of cake' for the Sopwith Schneider and its pilot Howard Pixton, lapping at a speed of almost 90 mph to destroy most of the opposition. Then, on the 15th lap, it turned into a cliff-hanger. The Schneider's engine began to misfire. After a few more laps, each of which seemed capable of taking years off Pixton's life expectation, he realized that (though rough and lacking in power) the engine was going to keep turning. He began to concentrate on the most meticulous flying to save every possible second of time. The tactics were good, and he won the contest at an average speed of 86.78 mph.

World War I prevented Britain staging the next contest until 1919, one expected to demonstrate that wartime development of aircraft and airframes had given an immense performance leap. Scheduled to take place off Bournemouth on 10 September 1919, frustrating fog made the event a washout. The Italian Sergeant Guido Janello in a Savoia S.13 completed the most laps, but his eleven were later ruled as invalid and the event was declared void. But as a gesture of goodwill, Italy was invited to host the next contest.

The first two of the next three events, staged at Venice, resulted in no international competition, with four Italian aircraft contending against each other but significantly raising the race speed to 107.22 mph in 1920 and 117.90 mph in 1921. But sudden realization that, in accordance with Jacques Schneider's rules, Italy now needed only one more win to capture the trophy permanently, a flurry of international activity to contend the event at Naples was stirred. The contest was now one of national prestige. Britain, France and Italy fielded aircraft, the British Supermarine Sea Lion II biplane flying-boat being specially prepared by the company's young designer, Reginald J. Mitchell, from the earlier Sea King Mk II.

Chosen to fly the Sea Lion II was Supermarine's chief test pilot, Henri Biard, who had recorded a very impressive speed of 150 mph in the aircraft before it was dismantled for transit to Naples. By then it was known that the French had withdrawn. Astutely, Biard did not demonstrate the Sea Lion's full potential during the pre-contest flight testing. When the race began, late in the afternoon of 12 August 1922, Biard alone stood between the three Italian contenders and a permanent home for the trophy in Italy. By luck Biard won the draw for starting position, and he

Right
Supermarine Sea Lion II flown by Henri Biard for the 1922 contest.

lifted cleanly off the water to record a first lap speed of more than 150 mph. This brought consternation to the Italians, who realized their Macchi M.7 and M.17 had little chance of winning. Their hopes, therefore, depended on the beautifully streamlined SIAI Savoia S.51, which, sadly, had suffered a ducking in the pre-race tests. What they had not appreciated was that the S.51's propeller had suffered from its immersion, the glue holding the wood laminations being softened and allowing some separation that was to cause vibration.

Spectators on the ground knew nothing of this, realizing only that the S.51, piloted by Alessandro Passaleva, was close behind the Sea Lion. Desperately Passaleva tried to use maximum engine power, edging ever closer to Biard but only being forced to pull back on the throttle to prevent what might be disastrous vibration. Biard won the event narrowly at an average speed of 145.7 mph. Britain had loosened Italy's hold on the trophy and would be responsible for hosting the next event. How lucky the Sea Lion II had been was demonstrated just over four months later, when Savoia's S.51 established a new world speed record for seaplanes at 174.08 mph.

The course for the 1923 contest was from Cowes, Isle of Wight, to a turning-point at Selsey Bill, Sussex, with Britain, France, Italy and the USA all hoping to field contenders. Italy was to

Left
Italy's Macchi M.17 stood little chance in the 1922 contest against the S.51 and Sea Lion II. (Aermacchi)

Left
Jimmy Doolittle standing on the float of the Curtiss R3C-2, 26 October 1925. (US Air Force)

Above
The beautifully streamline Macchi M.52 seaplane, which failed to finish the 1927 contest. (Aermacchi)

Below
Italian Macchi-Castoldi MC.72 and Macchi M.39 racers, the former which had not been ready in time to compete in the final Schneider Trophy event of 1931 but on 10 April 1934 established a new world speed record of 423.76 mph, which it bettered on 23 October. (Aermacchi)

to try and improve the M.39, resulting in the new designation Macchi M.52, while Fiat spent the year conjuring additional output from the AS.2 to produce the 1,000 hp AS.3. By not competing in the USA during 1926, Britain had enjoyed two years for preparation; the RAF had founded a High Speed Flight to train specialized pilots and the Air Ministry contracted new aircraft. These were the Gloster IV biplane, Short-Bristow Crusader ('Curious Ada' to the RAF) and Mitchell's superb Supermarine S.5. The S.5 benefited from Mitchell's experience with the S.4. It was a wonderfully sleek seaplane which, like the Macchi M.39/M.52, had the monoplane wings braced by streamline wires. It retained the same engine type as its Schneider Trophy predecessors, in this case a Napier Lion VII. The race itself proved to be a resounding British victory, even though 'Curious Ada' had crashed during a flight test because the aileron controls had been crossed over during re-erection. Two of the Macchi M.52s retired with engine failure in the first and second laps, the third M.52 with a fractured fuel line in the sixth lap, as did the Gloster IVB suffering from severe vibration. Only the two S.5s continued with their triumphant roar to the finishing line. with Flight Lieutenant S. N. Webster in first place at an average speed of 281.66 mph and Flight Lieutenant O. E. Worsley in second at 273.01 mph.

There had already been general realization that biennial competition would be necessary to allow adequate time for design and development. In consequence, the next (1929) contest was hosted by Britain with the starting- and finishing-point off Ryde Pier, Isle of Wight. Many contenders had been expected but in the final analysis it was Britain versus Italy, the latter fielding two Macchi M.67s with 1,400 hp engines plus the Macchi M.52R with a 1,000 hp AS.3. Supermarine provided Britain's hopes for success, an S.5 with a Napier Lion VIIB engine and two new and improved S.6 airframes, enlarged and strengthened to accept the new 1,900 hp Rolls-Royce 'R' engine.

All six aircraft came to the start in near perfect conditions on 7 September, but the M.67s were both to retire in the second lap from problems caused by their Isotta-Fraschini engines. This left only the M.52R to face the challenge of the Supermarines. British success came as all three completed the course, although Flight Officer R. L. R. Atcherley piloting one of the S.6s was disqualified for cutting a pylon. It was Flight Officer H. R. Waghorn in the other S.6 who won, at an average speed of 328.63 mph. Italy's Warrant Officer T. Dal Molin in the M.52R was second at 284.20 mph and Flight Officer D. D'Arcy Greig in the S.5 was third at 282.11 mph.

Britain now needed only to win in 1931 to secure the trophy, but a parsimonious government announced that it would not allocate the funds needed for participation. Despite pressure from many sources the government was adamant. But for the generous-hearted action of the patriotic and wealthy Lady Houston, who gave the Royal Aero Club a cheque for £100,000, it seems likely that British hopes of securing that third win would have been dashed for ever.

Both France and Italy intended to take part in the 1931 contest, again to be flown over the Solent, off the Isle of Wight. However, both were faced with serious problems in the development of their contending aircraft (including the loss of

Left
One of the two Supermarine
S.6Bs *S 1596* built to win the
trophy outright for Britain.

skilled pilots in high-speed crashes) and were unable to field their aircraft when the Royal Aero Club refused to postpone the contest date. The Club further underlined the refusal by stating that in the absence of competition a British aircraft would over-fly the course to take the trophy.

Thereby, on 13 September 1931, with only one of three members of the RAF's High Speed Flight needing to complete the course, the event was regarded as something of an anticlimax. Perhaps a few words from the pen of an eye-witness, F. D. Bradbrooke, writing in *The Aeroplane* of 16 September 1931, will add a little excitement and color to mere historic achievement:

'For three minutes from that moment [the start] there was real and patent excitement on Wittering Beach. A flea-like speck could be seen hopping from crest to crest on the Isle of Wight skyline. It decelerated and decreased to bare visibility, and the crowd buzzed to itself that Boothman had rounded the pylon and was approaching at six miles a minute.

Leading a faint smoke-trail he came. Half-a-mile away he began to turn, reached its peak in an ear-splitting vertical virage about 200 yards outside the pylon, and straightened evenly out to moan away down the coast . . . .

And so the show passed, and repassed, and was past. Seven times, almost as regularly as a planet in reverse, the whining speck came, howled about us and went . . . .

Finally, relayed over the microphone on Ryde Pier, came the triumphant clamour of 2,400 hp finishing the last Schneider Trophy Contest.'*

The Supermarine S.6B, flown by Flight Lieutenant J. N. Boothman at an average speed of 340.08 mph, had given Britain permanent possession of Jacques Schneider's trophy.

*Special thanks are given for permission to quote from *The Aeroplane*.

6

TO THE FROZEN ENDS OF THE EARTH

The first recorded attempt to reach the North Pole by air was made by three Swedish engineers, who lifted off from Spitzbergen on 11 July 1897 in the hydrogen balloon *Ornen* (Eagle). Three days later, perhaps predictably, it ended in disaster, and a further 33 years were to elapse before their bodies were discovered. By then, however, man had reached the Pole by air.

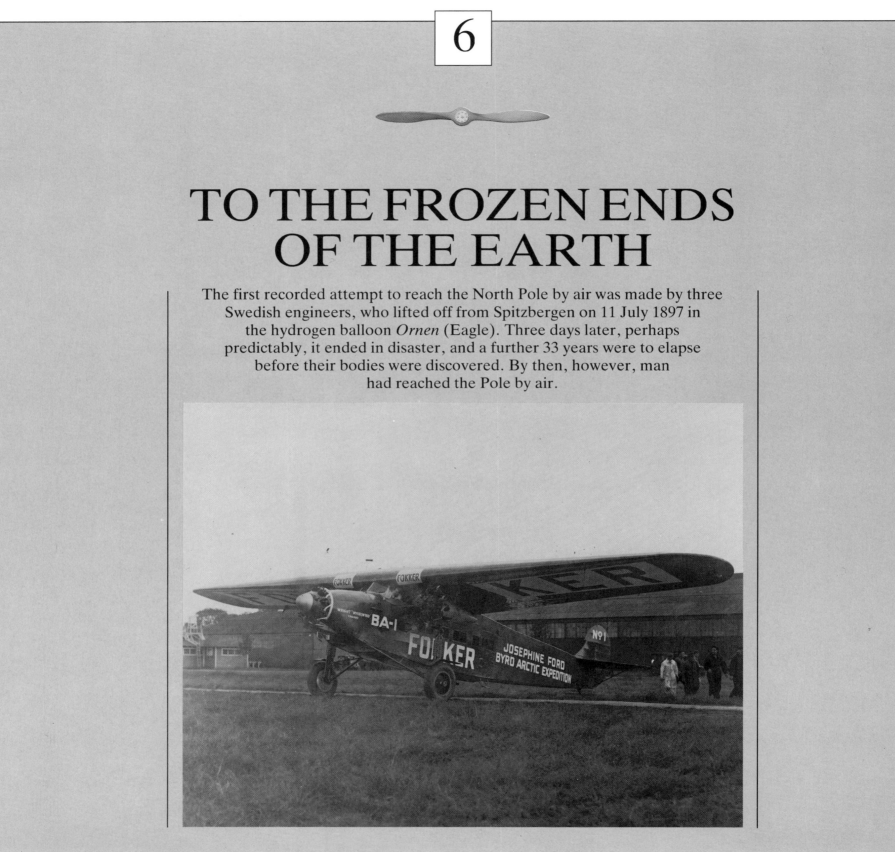

Left
Fokker F.VII-3m *Josephine Ford*
flown over the North Pole.
(US Department of the Navy)

Below
Amundsen's semi-rigid N.1
Norge airship.

But for a cruel stroke of luck, the honor of being first would surely have gone to the brilliant Norwegian explorer Roald Amundsen, who had already reached the South Pole on foot in 1911. After unsuccessful earlier attempts to fly to the North Pole, Amundsen and his American friend Lincoln Ellsworth, with two Norwegian pilots and two mechanics, took off from Kings Bay, Spitzbergen, in the late afternoon of 21 May 1925 in two twin-engined, open-cockpit Dornier Wal flying-boats numbered N.24 and N.25. All went well for seven hours, until one of N.25's engines failed. This aircraft made a safe landing, but N. 24 was holed by ice while making its own landing three miles away. On checking their positions, the two explorers discovered that they had come tantalizingly close to the required latitude — 87° 44' N — but that drift, which they were not equipped to measure accurately, had carried them 10° 20' W of their goal, leaving them still 136 miles from the Pole. They survived an incredible 16 days of hardship on the ice before, with its faulty engine repaired and all six men crowded on board, N.25 was able to lumber off the ice and fly them back to Spitzbergen.

Almost immediately, Amundsen and Ellsworth began to plan another attempt, this time by airship, and approached the Italian government to request use of the 670,980 cubic foot semi-rigid N.1 built by Colonel Umberto Nobile. This arrangement was approved by Mussolini on two conditions: that Nobile was appointed as airship commander, with five other Italians forming part of the crew, and that Italy would repurchase the N.1 if it survived the expedition in good condition. After being stripped, re-equipped and renamed *Norge*, the N.1 arrived in Spitzbergen on 7 May 1926, having had a four-week, 5,000-mile roundabout trip.

By that time, however, there was a serious rival already on the scene in the form of Lieutenant Commander Richard Evelyn Byrd of the US Navy, who was ready with his own attempt to reach the North Pole by airplane. Byrd was an experienced navigator and explorer. He had commanded one of the first US naval air stations (Halifax) in the Canadian Arctic in 1918, designed the navigation equipment for the USN's Curtiss NC transatlantic flying-boats of 1919, and taken part in the summer of 1925 in a 30,000 square mile aerial survey of northern Greenland. He had long had the ambition to reach the North Pole by air, and on 9 May 1926, only two days after the *Norge*'s arrival at King's Bay, he (as navigator) and his pilot Floyd Bennett, another early US naval aviator, flew to the Pole, circled it and returned, in a 1,600-mile round trip of about 15¾ hours. For such a flight, of course, a magnetic compass was useless, and navigating a trip of this length by sun compass, across hostile terrain in weather conditions in which the sun was rarely visible, was a remarkable tribute to Byrd's ability. In the circumstances, it may seem trite to describe the flight as uneventful, but the only scare was a slight oil leak in one engine.

The aircraft in which Byrd and Bennett flew was one with an unusual history. In the previous year Edsel Ford, of the celebrated motorcar company, had launched the Ford Reliability Tour, a 1,900-mile circuit of major US cities, to demonstrate the reliability of aircraft as a regular means of public transport. Dutchman Antony Fokker, whose American factory was producing a transport known as the F.VII, decided to enter this aircraft, but with its less than reliable single engine replaced by three more dependable, though lower-powered, units. Thus was born the F.VII-3m: the later-famous Fokker Tri-motor. The prototype dominated the Ford Tour, and after a brief period on loan to the US Army Air Service was purchased by Edsel Ford, named *Josephine Ford* after his daughter, designated BA-1 (Byrd Arctic No. 1), painted dark blue and donated to Byrd for his historic Polar flight. In recognition of their achievement both Byrd and Bennett were awarded the Congressional Medal of Honor; Byrd was also awarded the US Navy's Distinguished Service Medal.

Amundsen's efforts, although he was denied his cherished 'first' for a second time, did not go unrewarded. The *Norge* took off two days after *Josephine Ford*, remaining airborne (in a rather more eventful flight) for nearly three and a half days during which it passed over the Pole, continuing its journey to land at Teller, Alaska, on 14 May. Amundsen thereby achieved the first flight to traverse the Arctic completely. He and his helmsman, Oskar Wisting, also gained the well-deserved distinction of becoming the first men in history to visit both Poles. Despite some envelope damage, caused by lumps of ice flying off the propellers, the airship was largely unscathed, enabling Amundsen to claim the $46,000 'repurchase' price for returning it safely to Italian ownership.

Like Byrd's flight, that of the *Norge* was a remarkable feat of navigation and airmanship, but its achievement was sadly marred by some over-publicized personal differences between Amundsen and Nobile after the event. These were never settled directly. But when Nobile in his new airship *Italia* crashed in the Arctic two years later, Amundsen and his Norwegian pilot of 1925, Lief Dietrichson, volunteered to join the seven-nation aerial search for them. Tragically, although Nobile and seven of the *Italia's* 15-man crew were rescued, the only casualties among the would-be rescuers were Amundsen, Dietrichson and their four-man crew, whose aircraft crashed en route to Spitzbergen without even reaching the search area.

Meanwhile, Byrd, who had followed his North Polar flight by taking part in a transatlantic race the following year, had experienced no trouble in obtaining backers — including the US Navy — for his next Polar venture: a flight to the South Pole. Sadly, Bennett was to die from pneumonia before it could get underway, but not before he had made a major contribution to the plans for its execution.

Compared with the North Polar attempt, the Byrd Antarctic Expedition was a much larger, more difficult and more expensive operation. Unlike the Arctic, the Antarctic possessed no habitation within at least 1,000 miles of the South Pole, which meant that an entire operating base had to be established from scratch. A site was chosen in the Bay of Whales, on the edge of the Ross Sea about 800 miles from the Pole. It took 4 ships to ferry the equipment, more than 60 men and 4 aircraft from the USA to the new base, which was given the name Little America. In addition, since none of the aircraft was able to carry enough fuel for the round trip from Little America to the Pole and back, an auxiliary refuelling base was laid down near the foot of Mount Nansen, some 440 miles to the south of Little America.

For the flight attempt, Byrd chose a new tri-motor aircraft, this time a Ford 4-AT, naming it *Floyd Bennett* after his Arctic companion. He chose for his pilot Lieutenant Bernt Balchen of the Norwegian Army Air Service, a former member of Amundsen's Arctic expedition and the man who had designed and built new skis for the *Josephine Ford* after her original pair had been wrecked in early take-off attempts. Byrd was, again, in charge of both the flight and the navigation. Completing the *Floyd Bennett*'s crew were Harold I. June as radio operator, refueller and reserve pilot, and Captain Ashley C. McKinley of the US Navy as official aerial surveyor and photographer. McKinley's job, using a 100 lb Fairchild camera, was to map the flight path corridor between Little America and the Pole for the benefit of future expeditions.

Just before 4.00 pm (local time) on 28 November 1929, the

Ford tri-motor and its crew took off from McMurdo Sound in Little America. Included in the aircraft's 15,000 lb gross weight were two radio receivers and a transmitter, by means of which Harold June maintained hourly contact with their base. At the same time, progress of the flight was relayed from Little America to the *New York Times* radio station, enabling audiences in the United States to keep abreast of the event.

The first half of the outward leg passed without mishap, but then came a setback that could have cost all four men their lives. The flight path to the Pole involved climbing to cross the 10,000 foot Queen Maud range of mountains, by way of a 'valley' among the peaks created by the Axel Heiberg glacier. As they neared the mountains a fuel check revealed that the aircraft was too heavy to climb above the Heiberg — strong headwinds had caused fuel consumption to be much higher than they had calculated and so Balchen had kept the *Floyd Bennett* down to its most economical cruising speed and altitude. Weight had to be reduced, and quickly. Byrd knew that his decision could be, quite literally, one of life or death. If they jettisoned fuel, there would be too little left to complete the round trip back to Little America. If food was sacrificed, their chances of survival if forced to land would be seriously, perhaps fatally, compromised. Nevertheless, Byrd decided to throw out two 125 lb bags of food supplies. Balchen, meanwhile, had spotted a second glacier, the

Liv, alongside the Heiberg, which seemed to offer a slightly lower passage over the mountains, and the now-lightened Ford just managed to climb over the hump with a few hundred feet to spare.

Apart from a minor 'hiccup' in the starboard engine, caused by an over-lean fuel mixture that was soon corrected, no further problems were encountered. They overflew the Pole at about 1.15 on the morning of 29 November, dropping the flags of the United States (weighted by a stone from Floyd Bennett's grave), Great Britain, Norway and France. On the return flight, with their headwinds now transformed into tailwinds, they were able to outrun a snowstorm and touch down at the auxiliary depot to refuel. Within an hour they had taken off again, and arrived back in Little America less than 19 hours after they had left.

Byrd, who thus became the first man to fly over both Poles, was promoted from Commander to Rear Admiral a few weeks later, and was awarded the Navy Cross in recognition of his South Polar flight. In the Antarctic, which became his first love, he did much further flying and other exploration in the early part of the 1930s. His last visit was as adviser to 'Operation Deep Freeze I', the American contribution to the International Geophysical Year of 1957-8. Byrd's two historic Polar aircraft, the *Josephine Ford* and *Floyd Bennett*, are preserved to this day in the Henry Ford Museum at Dearborn, Michigan.

Below Left
Byrd testing a liferaft alongside the Lewis-Vought seaplane before the April 1925 McMillan polar expedition. (US Department of the Navy)

Below
Lieutenant Commander Richard Evelyn Byrd taking observations with the sextant used on the Arctic expedition. In the rear cockpit taking notes is Boatswain E. E. Rober. (US Department of the Navy)

fuselage was one giant tank. Further metal tanks occupied the inboard part of each wing. Together they housed the required 449 gallons, giving a design still-air range of 4,650 miles, greater than any airplane had ever had previously. When completed the gross weight was found to be 5,250 lb, which was certainly an awesome figure. Not least of the problems was that the cockpit, aft of the huge fuselage tank, had side windows but no forward view at all. The two-blade metal propeller had a huge spinner. This, and the entire metal skin of the forward fuselage, were buffed in a pattern that soon was to be famous all over the world. The rest of the aircraft was fabric covered, sprayed silver. It received experimental registration N-X-211, and on the nose was painted *Spirit of St Louis*.

Lindbergh made the first test flight on 28 April 1927. By this time there were plenty of others eager to win the Orteig prize: Commander Byrd, Clarence D. Chamberlin and several more. Coast to coast the newspapers drummed up a rather tawdry publicity, tending to focus on the tall loner from the Midwest. Soon the handsome yet poor young man was setting records, flying from the Ryan field across the great mountains to St Louis, despite severe icing, and then going on to Curtiss Field, New York. Here he had a carburetor heater fitted, but he still had no radio. In the cockpit were a turn/slip indicator, magnetic and Earth-inductor compasses and a drift sight. He planned meticulously, and relied totally on dead reckoning and on guessing the wind from the appearance of the sea.

Weather on 19 May was poor but it was expected to improve, so he decided to take off at dawn on the 20th. Unable to sleep, he was at the field at 2.15 am, relieved to find no sign of any rivals. In drizzling rain the NYP was then towed across to the new 5,000 foot strip at Roosevelt Field prepared by rival Byrd, who had given 'Lindy' — as the papers called him — permission to use it. Somehow not 449 but 451 gallons were laboriously poured in. Then, the thin tires almost sinking into the soggy grass, the throttle was opened fully for take-off. The NYP hardly moved, until everyone who was nearby began pushing on the wing struts. For 100 yards they pushed; even then the NYP was nowhere near getting the tail up and the rubber-sprung legs were bottoming on their stops with every bump. Ever so gradually the speed built up, until with each bump the silver airplane came nearer to flying. At the last moment Lindbergh was able to lift over some telegraph wires. One of the worst parts was over.

Soon the rain cleared, but over Nova Scotia the overloaded NYP bucked a violent storm for an hour. Almost 12 hours out he dived low over St John's, Newfoundland, crossing the field where Alcock and Brown had taken off eight years previously. Then he headed out over the wide Atlantic and into a moonless night. Increasingly his problem was a desperate need for sleep; or rather to stay awake. He had already had no sleep for 36 hours and still had almost another 24 hours to go. He wrote, 'The worst part about fighting sleep is that, the harder you fight, the more you strengthen your enemy and weaken your resistance to him.' Many times he awoke at the last moment as the aircraft fell off on one wing, and twice he found he was in a spiral dive. About 14 hours out he was so worried by icing that he even thought of turning back. Towering clouds all seemed to merge together in

Left
Spirit of St Louis at Camp Kearny parade ground after fuel-loading test flights. Aviation fuel was added to the aircraft in 50-US gallon increments. Charles Lindbergh is on the center bottom drum. (Ryan)

Below Left
Charles Augustus Lindbergh.

Below
The 46-foot span wing for the *Spirit* was built on the second floor of the Ryan Airlines factory at San Diego. It then had to be moved to the Ryan flying field at Dutch Flats, where the aircraft was assembled. (Ryan)

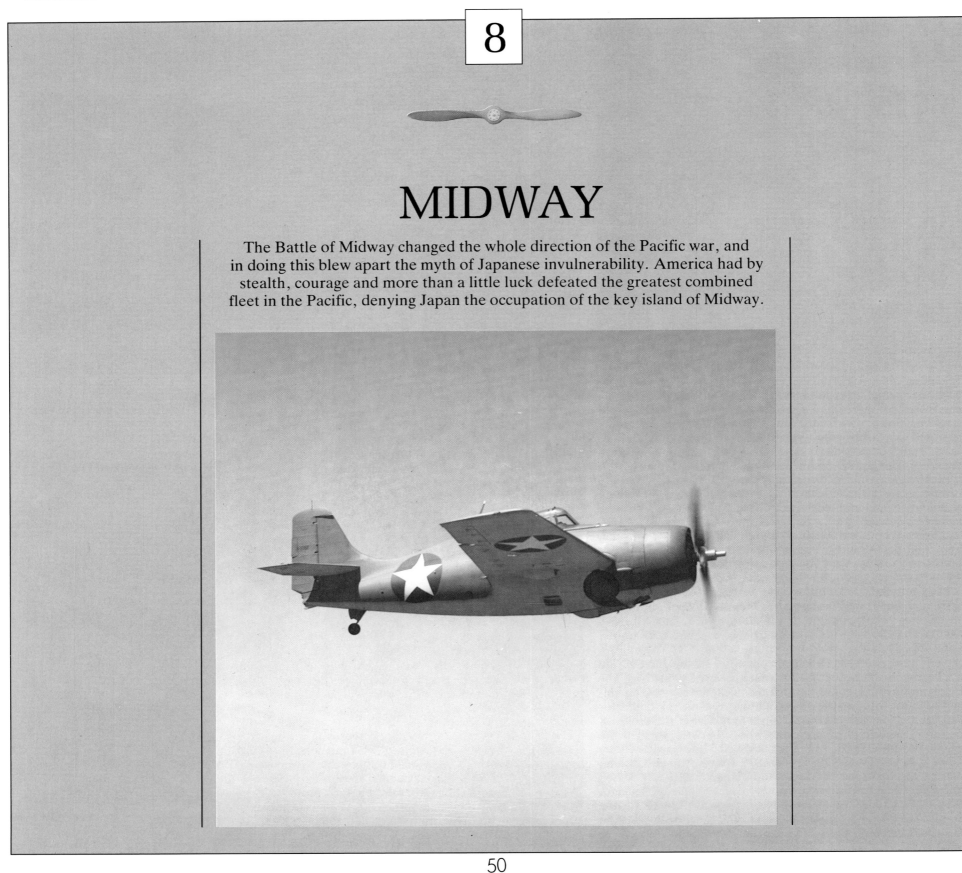

8

MIDWAY

The Battle of Midway changed the whole direction of the Pacific war, and in doing this blew apart the myth of Japanese invulnerability. America had by stealth, courage and more than a little luck defeated the greatest combined fleet in the Pacific, denying Japan the occupation of the key island of Midway.

But there is also a popular misconception that the battle left the Japanese without substantial aircraft carrier forces, so often are only the four carriers lost to Japan mentioned. Yet four other Japanese carriers survived the Midway and related Aleutian Islands actions. Furthermore, the large carrier *Shokaku* that had been damaged during the earlier Battle of the Coral Sea and *Zuikaku* went back into operational use, and the new *Hiyo* was commissioned.

American war games since 1928 had frequently demonstrated the vulnerability of shore defenses to surprise aircraft carrier attack, and in that very year aircraft from USS *Langley* mock raided the American Navy base at Pearl Harbor, Oahu (Hawaiian Islands). The defenders had been caught unaware, but had nothing more lethal than flour showered on them. Later exercises against Pearl Harbor before World War II met with comparable success.

The second generation US aircraft carriers were very much improved and faster and, in a highly significant speed trial by USS *Lexington* in June 1928, this carrier demonstrated an ability to sail from San Pedro to Honolulu in under 73 hours. But even this achievement was overshadowed in 1929. In a military exercise lasting 23-27 January, *Lexington* formed part of a fleet tasked with defending the Panama Canal against an 'attacking' force that included its sister ship *Saratoga* and a seaplane tender representing the unavailable first-generation *Langley*. In the early morning of the 26th, under the cover of darkness and in poor weather conditions, 70 fighters, bombers, scouts and a communications aircraft flew from *Saratoga*, together with a seaplane from the tender that singularly represented *Langley's* aircraft. Undetected, they pressed home their 'attack'. A second and smaller strike from *Saratoga* followed. The result was the theoretical annihilation of the Miraflores and Pedro Miguel locks and nearby airfields. From the point of view of the exercise, the Canal had been well and truly put out of action. But the surprises had not ended. Ironically, even before *Saratoga* had launched its second attack, it had been theoretically sunk several times over by 'enemy' battleships, aircraft and a submarine. A final twist came on the 27th, when naval land-based Martin bombers defending the Canal had seen their own carrier *Lexington* and, mistaking it for *Saratoga*, had 'sunk' this too. But out of the chaos came a sure and strong belief in the future of the aircraft carrier as an offensive naval vessel, with other warships contributing to *its* protection and not exclusively the other way around.

In February 1941 the US Navy established separate Atlantic and Pacific Fleets, although the likelihood of an attack on American assets in the Pacific were deemed insignificant. As if to reinforce this attitude, Alaskan Defense Command of the then

US Army Air Corps (tasked in part with defending certain Pacific naval bases in the north) seemed doomed to be the last to receive modern replacement aircraft. That was a mistake!

On 7 December 1941 America's fighting neutrality was shattered. While radios played music around the island at Pearl Harbor on this quiet Sunday morning, like a beacon in the Pacific Ocean, Imperial Japanese Navy Mitsubishi A6M2 Zero-Sen fighters, Aichi D3A1 dive-bombers and Nakajima B5N2 bombers and torpedo-bombers had been mustering in the skies. At 7.55 am they made their opening surprise strike against the resting American ships, airfields and other targets. The attacking aircraft, and the second wave, came from six Japanese aircraft carriers belonging to a fleet that had approached unheeded. The total offensive force was some 350 aircraft. A small but significant strength of fighters had also been kept back for defense, and floatplanes flew from cruisers and battleships. The destruction to American battleships and land-based aircraft was immense. But the US carriers of the Pacific Fleet had by chance escaped the onslaught, with *Enterprise* then returning from Wake Island, *Lexington* sailing to Midway, and *Saratoga* still in San Diego following maintenance.

In essence the Pearl Harbor raid had been a huge success for Japan, judged by the destruction of US assets. The warplanes led by Commander Mitso Fuchida had incredibly surprised the Americans fully, and he had sent this news back to Admiral Nagumo by the now famous phrase 'Tora, Tora, Tora'. But the absence of the American aircraft carriers, and so their continued survival for future battles, had been a bad blow for the attackers. This was compounded by their failure to destroy five submarines and their base, the fuel and oil complex, the harbor's power system and the naval repair facilities. The next day the USA declared war on Japan.

Japanese military victories quickly mounted, against which the Allies achieved only spasmodic results. *Enterprise* and *Yorktown* opened the American carrier offensive by striking at Japanese installations in Kwajalein, Jaluit, Makin, Mili, Wake and Wotje islands in February 1942, but for the loss of *Langley* (then no longer classed as an operational aircraft carrier) on the 27th while ferrying fighters to Java. On 18 April a daring propaganda raid on Tokyo and other Japanese targets was successfully achieved by American Mitchell bombers flying a one-way mission off the carrier USS *Hornet*, most landing in friendly China. The actual damage caused was small, but it made Japan fearful of further raids.

Then came the first real test. Japan had intended to land forces

Above Left
The Mitsubishi A6M Zero-Sen was without question the finest fighter of the early Pacific war years.

Left
Intended for ship use, the Grumman Avenger made its operational debut from land during the Battle of Midway. A bomber and torpedo plane, it also carried machine-guns for defense in a power-operated dorsal turret, rearward facing ventral position and forward firing. (Grumman Corporation)

at Port Moresby (New Guinea), using aircraft carriers (under command of Vice Admiral Shigeyoshi Inouye) to provide air cover and air attack forces. Working on good intelligence and thereby assuming the threat, between 4 and 8 May *Yorktown* and *Lexington* in company with other ships engaged the Japanese in what became known as the Battle of the Coral Sea. Initial targets for the Douglas Dauntless and Devastator bombers/torpedo bombers and Grumman Wildcat fighters from *Yorktown* were ships engaged in landings at Tulagi Harbor, including transports, minesweepers and a destroyer. On the 5th the two US carrier forces joined up south of the Louisiade Archipelago in the Coral Sea. That same night the Japanese carriers *Shokaku* and *Zuikaku* of the strike force approached and then headed for the Japanese invasion transport fleet. As soon as it was realized quite how close the US carriers were, the invasion fleet was turned away and Port Moresby reprieved. But this was just the beginning.

On the 7th, US aircraft found and sank the carrier *Shoho* of the invasion force. The following day a battle royal took place. Near simultaneous air attacks on opposing US and Japanese carriers left the *Lexington* so badly damaged and on fire that it had to be abandoned and was finally deliberately sunk by torpedoes from a friendly destroyer. *Yorktown* too had been hit by a bomb, but survived. Meanwhile US aircraft had struck at the carrier *Shokaku*, leaving it damaged and requiring weeks to repair.

Left
Admiral Chester Nimitz on Midway Island, on the occasion of presenting awards to Navy and Marine Corps personnel who had helped repel Japanese flying-boats on the night of 10 March 1942.
(US Department of the Navy)

Below Left
Lieutenant Colonel James 'Jimmy' Doolittle led a daring 16 aircraft raid on Tokyo, Nagoya, Yokohama, Yokosuka and Kobe on 18 April 1942, the North American B-25 Mitchells flying from USS *Hornet*. (US Air Force)

Below
Damage on Sand Island, Midway, after the Japanese air attacks of 4 June. (US Department of the Navy)

Above
Curtiss P-40 Warhawks from Umnak took their toll of Japanese aircraft during the Aleutian campaign.

Above Right
The only Grumman TBF Avenger to survive the attack on the Japanese aircraft carriers on 4 June was Burt Earnest's, and even in this a gunner was killed and two of the other three crew wounded. (Grumman Corporation)

So ended the first ever naval battle involving fleets not in direct contact, and the first to be decided by air power alone. The outcome was indecisive. Both Japan and the USA had lost a carrier and both had another badly damaged. Other vessels of each side had fallen victim too, including destroyers. In total the US lost 69 carrier aircraft that day, more than half going down on the *Lexington*. The Imperial Japanese Navy lost 43 aircraft during the battle operations plus others thrown over the side of *Zuikaku* to make space for aircraft unable to land back on *Shokaku*. For the engagement as a whole a number of other US aircraft had been lost, but these were fewer than *Shoho's* losses.

With the threatened invasion of Port Moresby defeated and many experienced Japanese airmen lost, the Battle of the Coral Sea has to be seen as an Allied victory, not least as this had resulted in the first major setback for the Japanese invasion forces in the war. But the Japanese still had nine important aircraft carriers in the Pacific plus escort carriers. Another confrontation with US carrier forces was inevitable.

Japanese eyes turned to the islands of Midway and the far off Aleutians to the north, where branches of all three American services were stationed. Midway was the greater prize. Midway also held the key to the eventual capture of Pearl Harbor, offering the prospect of both an early-warning base on US movements and a springboard for an offensive. But the plan was more than merely the capture of the island. By drawing the battle-mauled US Pacific Fleet into conflict against a vastly larger Japanese force, it was intended to deal a crushing blow that would effectively end US power in the region and make capture of Oahu inevitable. And with the British tied up in their own actions, there was no prospect of assistance in time. American Atlantic Fleet carriers were also beyond call. To guarantee further the defeat of the US Pacific Fleet, submarines were to be provided to block routes to Midway and the north. However, in the event the US ships were not troubled by these submarines.

The plan was multifold. Some 1,500 miles to the north of Midway lay the Aleutian Islands, stringing out from Alaska in a sweeping arc. Dutch Harbor on the island of Unalaska held an important US Navy base. The defeat of this base and the occupation of Adak, Attu and Kiska islands in the western sector of the chain would not only give Japan a foothold close to the American continent but would also make more difficult any American plans to muster a force to attack Japan in the near future (Japan was then still smarting from Doolittle's carrier raid on Tokyo in April). Furthermore, the occupation was intended to form the northern link in a defensive string of islands to protect Japan that could stretch all the way down to the Coral Sea off the Australian coast. Finally, but importantly, it was hoped that the Americans on Midway and Pearl Harbor would be diverted by the slightly earlier pre-emptive Aleutian attack.

For the Aleutian operation a Japanese fleet under Vice Admiral Hosogaya included the carriers *Junyo* and *Ryujo*, 13 destroyers, 7 cruisers, 6 submarines, a minelayer, 5 transports and 5 auxiliary vessels. For the actual Midway operation, the Japanese assembled three naval elements under the overall command of Admiral Yamamoto. One element comprised the principal carriers *Akagi, Hiryu, Kaga* and *Soryu*, plus 17 other warships, intended chiefly to knock out the American defenses on Midway and offer cover against US attacks. The second was the invasion force, with 16 transports and other auxiliary ships supported by the light carrier *Zuiho* and 41 warships. Finally came Yamamoto's own group, with the carrier *Hosho*, 34 warships plus auxiliary vessels. The seaplane carriers sailing with the elements were integral to the operation.

To oppose a Midway attack, the US had its shore-based USAAF and Marine Corps/Navy aircraft and a naval force which included the carriers *Enterprise* and *Hornet* of Task Force 16, supported by 17 cruisers and destroyers, and the carrier *Yorktown* of Task Force 17, supported by 8 cruisers and destroyers. The fact that *Yorktown* was available for battle at all reflected Japan's mistake at the time of the Pearl Harbor attack in not destroying the repair facilities on that island. It would cost Japan dearly. Rear Admiral F. J. Fletcher had overall charge of

the carrier groups, with Rear Admiral R. A. Spruance subordinately commanding TF 16. In overall US command of operations was Admiral Chester Nimitz on Pearl Harbor. Fortunately, America had good intelligence gathering, and reports left Nimitz in no doubt that Midway was the main Japanese goal.

To the north, the defense of and around the Aleutians centered on inadequate US Navy warships and old submarines, Army units, plus USAAF bombers and fighters based at airfields from Nome on the Seward Peninsula of Alaska to the islands of Kodiak and Umnak under Alaskan Defense Command. By the time of the Dutch Harbor attack the US Navy had some 25 surface warships and submarines in the immediate area, with the USAAF tasked to protect the naval bases at Dutch Harbor, Kodiak and elsewhere. The Umnak base was the furthest out, 65 miles from Dutch Harbor, thereby suiting both outer point defense and offensive operations. The air strength of some 140 aircraft immediately available from bases in the Aleutians and southern Alaska at the time of the Dutch Harbor attack represented a rapid last-minute expansion and modernization. This strength came under the auspices of the Eleventh Air Force. Fighters included Lockheed P-38 Lightnings, Bell P-39 Airacobras and Curtiss P-40 Warhawks, forming the bulk of the total force, while bombs and torpedoes could be dropped from Boeing B-17 Flying Fortresses and Martin B-26 Marauders among other less important types that included a Liberator. The Navy also had 23 Catalina armed patrol flying-boats, which proved essential in spotting Japanese ships.

Japanese operations against Dutch Harbor began on 3 June, but the poor weather conditions that had helped them close in undetected also initially hampered their operations. Some carrier aircraft launched for the initial strike on the 3rd returned without action, although six fighters pressed home a strafing attack, followed within minutes by small waves of bombers. A second strike launched to hit US warships turned back because of the weather conditions. Of four Aichi E13A1 seaplanes flown off

the cruisers *Maya* and *Takao* to make a reconnaissance, one was shot down by a P-40 of the 11th Fighter Squadron from the still secret Umnak airfield. So far the Japanese had lost four aircraft, and the Americans two Catalina flying-boats.

On the 4th heavier Japanese attacks on Dutch Harbor caused substantial damage. In return, after a Catalina of Patrol Wing 4 had spotted and reported Japanese ships, including at least one carrier, USAAF B-17 and B-26 bombers attacked the Japanese vessels, but without success. However, Curtiss P-40 fighters flying from Umnak had claimed another four Japanese aircraft as they had rendezvoused unknowingly over the US fighter base. So, the day ended with five Japanese air losses, while the USAAF had lost two P-40 fighters, a B-17, two B-26s and one

Consolidated LB-30 Liberator II (that had originally been destined, with others, for the RAF but had been repossessed and was attached to 36 Squadron flying mostly B-17s). The US Navy Catalinas had suffered a worse fate in the air and while stationary, and only 14 remained airworthy. On the 7th a Japanese force occupied the undefended islands of Attu and Kiska, which they held for about a year.

Meanwhile, US long-range aircraft had been patrolling from Midway in an attempt to detect the expected Japanese. On the morning of the 3rd a Catalina spotted ships. That afternoon USAAF B-17s bombed Japanese transport ships from high level, but without success.

Soon after 1.00 am on the 4th a Catalina struck a Japanese auxiliary with a torpedo. Only hours later the main Japanese attacks on Midway began. Flying from the four main carriers that were still well over 200 miles from Midway, incoming Japanese aircraft were detected by Midway's radar, while the same Japanese carriers had also been seen by patrolling Catalinas. Defending US Midway-based Buffalo and Wildcat fighters were outgunned and outmatched, and for a devastating 30 minutes from 6.30 am Japanese warplanes carried out heavy raids on military installations.

As the Japanese aircraft were beginning their return flight from the attack, six American Grumman Avengers and four B-26 Marauders from Midway began retaliation against the ships. The Avengers of VT-8 (Torpedo Squadron 8) had only arrived on Midway on 1 June, having flown originally from Norfolk Naval Air Station to Pearl Harbor with the intention of joining the rest of VT-8 flying Devastators on board *Hornet*. But, while the Avenger later achieved outstanding success as a carrier bomber, this early morning debut ended tragically, and only one limped back to Midway together with just two of the twin-engined Marauders. Now came a fateful decision. Vice Admiral Nagumo, commanding the carrier divisions as he had for Pearl Harbor, ordered the attack aircraft on *Akagi* and *Kaga* to have their anti-ship torpedoes replaced by bombs, allowing for a second massive strike on Midway. While this was being organized word came of approaching US warships. The order to rearm was arrested, the aircraft once again needed for ship attack. Further unsuccessful attacks by American Midway-based B-17s, Dauntless and Vindicator dive-bombers also followed. However, Japanese warplanes now closing in on their home carriers after the first Midway strike needed to be recovered. Room had to be made on deck, although rearming was still in progress. Vital time had been lost. Presently, work once again got underway to arm and fuel the Japanese attack aircraft force. But now incoming American carrier aircraft were located. Zero fighters were dispatched to intercept but still the decks were

Right
On 6 June American carrier aircraft attacked the Japanese cruisers *Mikuma* (as seen here, which sank) and *Mogami* (which, despite appalling damage, was saved and repaired). (US Department of the Navy)

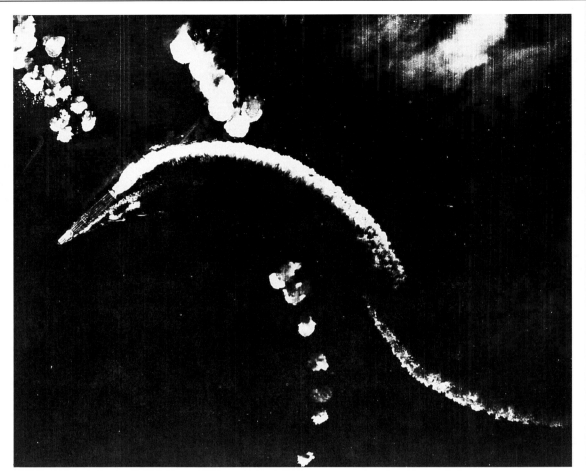

covered with other unready warplanes.

The incoming American attack force, however, comprised only 15 outdated Douglas Devastators of VT-8 from the *Hornet*. A very much larger attack force had been dispatched from the US carriers but had been unable to find the relocated Japanese vessels, and some had even run out of fuel and ditched in the sea. Valiantly the Devastators went in unescorted. They were cut to ribbons. Not a single aircraft survived, and only one crewman. Some help might have been expected from a number of Wildcats flying high above, but these had not been signalled. Almost immediately after, however, VT-6 from *Enterprise* attempted the same attack, followed by VT-3 from *Yorktown*. Only four from VT-6 survived. The American carriers had lost their force of Devastators. Moreover, VT-8 had not only been lost from the carrier force, but its intended Avenger replacements had been destroyed also in that earlier attack from land.

A Japanese counter-strike was ordered. Meanwhile, the other remaining airborne American aircraft had been searching for their targets. Having been launched some time after 7.00 am, the Dauntless bombers from *Enterprise* were running dangerously low on fuel. But presently they sighted three Japanese carriers. As so little time had elapsed since the Devastator raids, Japanese defenses and fighters were looking generally low for torpedo aircraft, allowing the high diving Dauntless bombers to close virtually unhindered. *Akagi* and *Kaga* were singled out, their decks covered with aircraft, bombs and fuel. Both ships were left burning and destroyed. Almost immediately Dauntless bombers from *Yorktown* flew in, attacking and destroying *Soryu*. By 10.30 am three of the four main Japanese carriers had been lost, and in the space of about five minutes! *Kaga* and *Soryu* sank in the early evening of that day. The other crippled carrier was torpedoed by its own ships on the morning of the 5th.

Just 10 minutes after the American raids, *Hiryu* launched a counter-attack against the alerted *Yorktown*. Although the Japanese aircraft were badly shot up, some Aichi D3A dive-bombers found their target. A second strike in the afternoon caused more damage. This time the unlucky carrier was nearing its end. Then still salvageable, it was finally struck by two torpedoes from a Japanese submarine and sank on the 7th. Another of the submarine's torpedoes fired at the same time hit the destroyer USS *Hammann*, which sank immediately. By the afternoon of the 4th *Hiryu* too had been successfully hit and sunk by US carrier planes from *Enterprise*, although B-17s from Midway had joined in. Without control of the air, the Japanese had no choice but to withdraw. US attacks from Midway on the 5th and from US carriers on the 6th brought a further loss to the Japanese, when the cruiser *Mikuma* was sunk by carrier aircraft.

The war had turned irretrievably against the Japanese, which relied on command of the seas. Japan's intention had been to win early battles by surprise and overwhelming strength, giving its enemies little time to reinforce or manufacture new equipment because, as a nation, Japan itself had not the manufacturing output to sustain heavy equipment losses. But, as yet, it was not defeated, and to the surviving carriers could be added *Shokaku* and *Zuikaku* which had been put out of the Midway force by their experiences during the Battle of the Coral Sea. The invaders had lost 4 carriers, 258 aircraft and a cruiser. By contrast, the vastly outnumbered US fleet had lost only *Yorktown* and a destroyer, plus a little over 100 carrier aircraft. A further 40 shore-based US warplanes had been destroyed.

Final Allied victory in the Pacific would still take three years.

9

DESPERATE MEASURES

As any dictionary tells, the word 'great' has many meanings. For most of the stories told in *Great Moments in Aviation* it conveys 'exceptional achievement'. For this story, however, it means something entirely different, perhaps best defined as 'significant importance'. For this is a story of tragedy, of war at its most horrific, yet as significant in the annals of aviation history as any of the others told here.

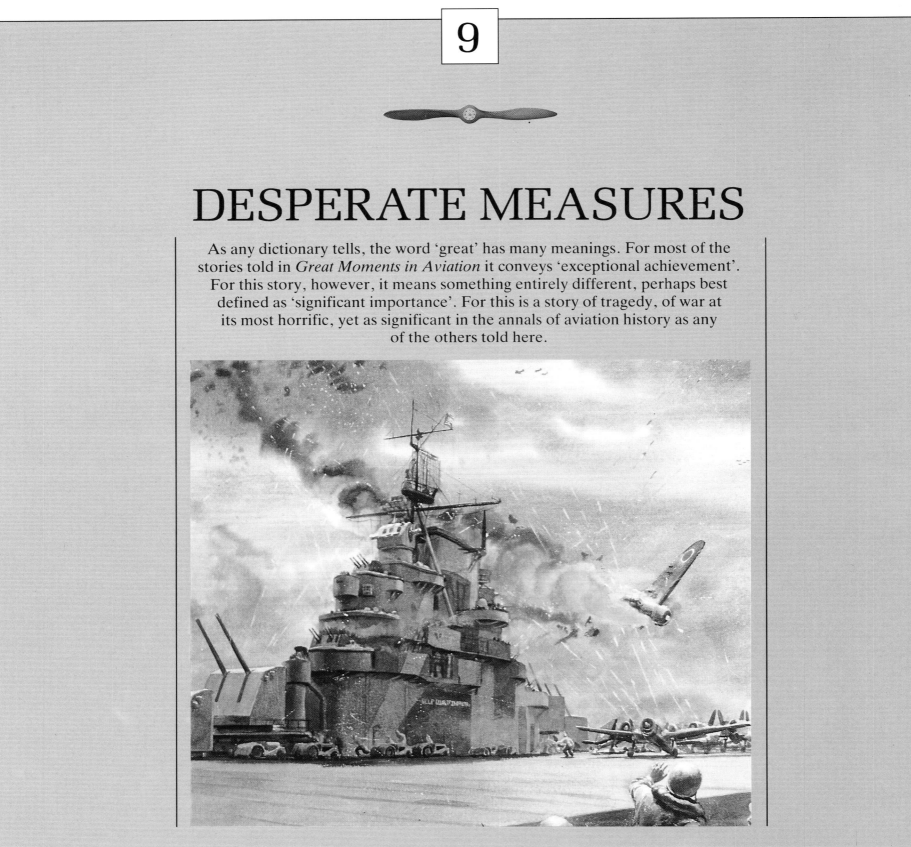

Below
USAAF Mitchell bomber of the
38th Bomber Group, 5th Air
Force, making an attack on an
enemy transport ship carrying
cargo to the Japanese at Ormoc,
Leyte.

Left
Kamikaze by Dwight Shepler.
(US Department of the Navy)

Below
USAAF Mitchell bomber of the
38th Bomber Group, 5th Air
Force, making an attack on an
enemy transport ship carrying
cargo to the Japanese at Ormoc,
Leyte.

Bottom
The closing seconds of a
Japanese Kamikaze attack on
USS Louisville. (US Department
of the Navy)

By mid-1944 the Japanese forces on the ground, at sea and in the air were buckling under the growing weight and success of the Allies fighting the Pacific campaign. The sea provided Japan's main lifeline between home and the conquered territories spread over vast distances. But since the US Navy had gained the initiative in the period following the great Battle of Midway, the situation for Japan had grown increasingly more desperate. To compound this, Japan had not only lost Admiral Isoroku Yamamoto (Commander-in-Chief of the Combined Fleet) on 18 April 1943 in a mid-air ambush by USAAF P-38G Lightning fighters of 339 Squadron, but also his successor, Admiral Koga, in a flying-boat accident on 31 March 1944.

In late 1943 fighter pilots of the Imperial Japanese Navy had suggested the idea of making suicide attacks in their aircraft on Allied ships, guaranteeing greater 'hit' accuracy than merely dropping bombs or torpedoes. At the time the situation had not demanded such sacrifice and the plan was declined, but in 1944 it was again raised as a possible solution to Allied naval strength.

On 10 October 1944 the US campaign opened for the occupation of Leyte, starting with massive air attacks on Japanese airfields on Okinawa and the Ryukyus, then Luzon, Formosa and around Manila. No fewer than 17 American aircraft carriers plus supporting vessels were employed, witnessing the destruction of more than 800 Japanese aircraft, 438 in the air. The actual occupation of Leyte began on 20 October, supported by further massive carrier forces. A huge Japanese fleet attempted to hamper the landings but was opposed by elements of the US Third and Seventh Fleets, and the Battle for Leyte Gulf erupted between 23-26th while other related actions raged. It was during the Battle for Leyte Gulf that the Japanese finally introduced suicide attacks, best remembered as Kamikaze, sinking the US Navy escort carrier St Lo and damaging six others. But these battles also saw the destruction of the Japanese fleet as an effective fighting force, and it limped away short of 26 light aircraft carriers, battleships, destroyers and cruisers. The Japanese had also lost a vast number of aircraft. In the fighting that followed more losses were inflicted on Japan, but in return between 29 October and 25 November seven US carriers were hit by Kamikaze planes.

As the war situation became even worse for the Japanese forces, so greater numbers of suicide attacks were staged, with conventional warplanes being joined later by rocket-powered and air-launched Yokosuka MXY7 Ohkas (Cherry Blossom). The Ohka's opening attack had, however, been a disaster. On 21 March 1945 Ohkas of the 721st Kokutai had headed into battle under their 16 launching Mitsubishi G4M2e bomber 'motherplanes', but were intercepted and released by desperate

aircrews too far away from their targets. But success was just around the corner. This came on 1 April, when the battleship USS *West Virginia* was one of four ships struck and damaged. The first Allied loss to an Ohka happened 11 days later, when the destroyer USS *Mannert L. Abele* was sunk off Okinawa. It is thought that by the time the last Kamikaze sortie took place on 15 August 1945, by seven aircraft of the Oita Detachment, 701st Air Group led by Admiral Matome Ugaki, some 2,257 Kamikaze sorties had been flown, of which 936 aircraft had returned to base without finding targets (something no Ohka pilot could do once released). Of 322 US Navy ships alone hit by Kamikaze planes, however, only 34 were sunk.

In contrast to Japan, the Allies had little need for desperate measures in the later war years. But five years after the war had begun a decision taken by the recently installed President of the United States, Harry S. Truman, and his advisers had an element of desperation about it. The decision was to drop atomic bombs on Japan.

Historians and others have long debated the justifications for this, if indeed there were any, and this is something not even hindsight can solve. Perhaps 225,000 Japanese were killed or injured in the two attacks, with other deaths later, a terrible result of world war. But, many argue that without the two bombs the fighting would have continued into 1946, leading to a full-scale invasion of Japan and causing the universally accepted estimates of one million Allied casualties and four million Japanese. The effects of the two nuclear weapons have horrified everyone for the past 43 years, but without them it is also universally believed that either the Berlin Crisis of 1948, the Korean War of the early 1950s or the Vietnam War might have seen the use of such awesome weapons. The most important legacy of Hiroshima and Nagasaki has been that no nation has since used such a weapon and the world knows none must.

The development of what at the time was called the 'atom bomb', and which today we would describe as the first nuclear

Top Left
Comrades cheer a bomb-laden Zero-Sen fighter about to take off from a Philippine airfield on a Kamikaze mission, October-November 1944. (US Department of the Navy)

Above
A Japanese Yokosuka D4Y Suisei hit by anti-aircraft fire from USS *Wasp* off the Ryukyus. (US Department of the Navy)

Left
Damaged aircraft on USS *Randolph* after a Kamikaze attack near the Caroline Islands. (US Department of the Navy)

Above
USS *Saratoga* after sustaining a Kamikaze attack on 21 February 1945. (US Department of the Navy)

Top Right
Japanese Zero-Sen maneuvers to make a Kamikaze attack on USS *Missouri*, 28 April 1945. It missed. (US Department of the Navy)

Right
Personal notes being written on 2,000 lb bombs about to be loaded on a Boeing B-29 Superfortress targeted for Japan. (US Air Force)

weapons, stemmed from a letter written by the great physicist Albert Einstein to President Roosevelt in 1939. Einstein warned that Nazi Germany's research into nuclear physics could result in the development of a bomb thousands of times more powerful than anything previously possible. The President eventually agreed to an investigation of the possibility of developing such a weapon. In Britain work had already begun, and British physicists made a big contribution to what was called The Manhattan Project.

At first work centered on the fissionable (splittable) property of atoms of the rare isotope of uranium U-235, but later it was found plutonium Pu-239 could also be used. Pu-239 never existed in nature, and to separate out U-235 required colossal plants costing hundreds of millions of dollars, as well as astronomic amounts of electric power. By summer 1944 there was little doubt bombs of both types could be constructed. The overall director, Brigadier-General Leslie R. Groves, thereupon ordered the establishment of a special unit to deliver the bombs. There was never any question that the unit would be part of the US Army Air Forces, that the aircraft would be the Boeing B-29 Superfortress, and that the target would be Japan.

General Henry H. Arnold, Chief of Staff, put the wheels in motion and picked a B-17 veteran, Colonel Paul W. Tibbets Jr, as commander of the special force. In September 1944 the choice fell on a new B-29 unit which was training at Fairmont Field, Nebraska: the 393rd Bomb Squadron of the 504th Bomb Group. It was detached from the 504th, flown to a remote base at Wendover, Utah, and engaged in an unprecedented program of training. Everyone knew it was special, and it clearly involved a special kind of bomb. By the time the 393rd had formed the core of the 509th Composite Group on 17 December 1944 everyone knew they would carry a single bomb of large size and weighing about 10,000 lb, would drop it from 30,000 feet and then get 'as far from the target as possible as fast as possible'. Outside the 509th not a whisper leaked out.

Tibbets alone knew what their missions would be. He quickly formed his own crew from men who had impressed him during his service, including Major Tom Ferebee, bombardier, and Captain Theo van Kirk, navigator. In May 1945 the 509th, from the start an isolated and totally self-sufficient unit, re-equipped with B-29s newly delivered from Martin's Omaha plant. They had no guns except in the tail, various items of special equipment and reversing propellers. By early June the elite crews were gathering at North Field, Tinian, in the liberated Marshall Islands, which was already home to the 21st Bomber Command led by General Curtis LeMay. Here the 509th aircraft aroused much speculation. They were all painted in spurious markings of other groups, notably the circled R of the 6th, and they occupied a special remote compound. Constantly under guard, they were used for training day and night. The norm was for trainee B-29 crews to make 20 practise bomb runs (if they were lucky). The 509th's normal was 1,000. Throughout, not one B-29 nor one crew member was lost, despite countless missions with live conventional high-explosive bombs against the small Japanese-held island of Rota.

Back in Washington there was some shuffling of the special target list, but at the top came the city of Hiroshima, easily identifiable and with no Allied prisoner-of-war camp nearby. The scientists at Los Alamos were confident that the U-235 bombs would work, but had slight doubts about the Pu-239 system with its complex fusing and implosion devices. Accordingly, a plutonium bomb was detonated on top of a tall steel mast in the remote desert at Alamogordo, on 16 July 1945. The explosion 'yield' was the expected 20 kilotons (ie, similar to 20,000 tons of TNT). From that day the world had a terrifying new weapon.

On 1 August the first uranium bomb, called *Little Boy*, was assembled at Tinian. It was closely followed by the first plutonium bomb, *Fat Man*, so called because its girth was tailored exactly to fit the B-29's cavernous bomb bay. Following Japanese rejection of Allied surrender pleas, the US President

Above
All but two B-29s used only conventional bombs against Japan during Pacific operations. Here *Dina Might* awaits its next mission. (Boeing)

Right
Bockscar, the B-29 that struck Nagasaki. (US Air Force)

Far Right
Fat Man, the nuclear bomb dropped on Nagasaki. (Los Alamos Scientific Laboratory)

authorized the first mission. By this time the Japanese were used to high-altitude day attacks by small groups of 509th aircraft, so the mission of Monday, 6 August 1945, excited little interest. First off, at midnight, was a weather reconnaissance B-29. Then came a standby aircraft which went ahead to wait at Iwo Jima. Following on were two B-29s heading via Hiroshima for other targets, Kokura and Nagasaki. At 2.45 am Tibbets took off in his own aircraft, *44-86292*, named after his mother *Enola Gay*. At beyond maximum weight, he had full fuel and *Little Boy* on board. Minutes later North Field reverberated to the sound of *Necessary Evil* (Major George Marquardt) to take photos and *The Great Artiste* (Major Charles W. Sweeney, CO of the 393rd) packed with scientific instruments, some of which were dropped near the target.

En route to Hiroshima the bomb was armed by Captain William Parsons USN and Lieutenant Morris Jeppson, who had passed a special training course at Los Alamos. Ferebee began his bomb run 28 miles out and at 8.15 am local time *Little Boy* was released at 328 mph and 31,600 feet. Immediately Tibbets put the B-29 into a maximum-rate diving turn through 150° and at full throttle raced away. Tibbets alone of the crew forgot to put on special protective spectacles. Less than a minute later the bomb exploded, about five miles away on the map and six miles below, 1,900 feet above the city. 'Brighter than a thousand Suns', the bomb almost immediately killed 80,000 and badly injured 50,000 more. Over 60,000 buildings were destroyed, the devastation over five square miles being total. The interior of *Enola Gay* was illuminated unnaturally by the brilliant fireball of 8,000 feet across. The mushroom cloud rose to over 50,000 feet and the aircraft was hit by two powerful shock waves. The tailgunner could still see the cloud 363 miles away.

The realization that a city had been destroyed by a single bomb struck a new fear into the Japanese leaders, but no message of surrender was sent by them. Accordingly, a mission was mounted against the second city on the list, Kokura. Tibbets picked Major Sweeney for this mission, and at 2.30 am on 9

August he and his handpicked crew took off from North Field in B-29 *(44-27297) Bockscar*. On board was the enormous plutonium bomb *Fat Man*. There was dense cloud over Kokura. With conventional bombs a run could have been made on radar, but on these special missions visual sighting was mandatory. Sweeney therefore headed for the secondary target, Nagasaki (which had replaced the original choice, Yokohama). Here again there was cloud cover, but just as an abort was being discussed a small clear patch appeared and grew. An accurate run was made and *Fat Man* was released at 10.50 local time from 28,900 feet. This time the steep undulations of the city shielded large areas, casualties amounting to 95,000 of which 35,000 were deaths. On the next day the Soviet Union declared war on Japan, and surrender negotiations began almost immediately.

On 2 September, surrounded by ships of the US Third Fleet, Japanese surrender documents were signed on board the battleship *USS Missouri* anchored in Tokyo Bay. Even then US aircraft carriers were on guard just in case the surrender was part of a cunning Japanese ambush. It wasn't. World war was over.

Above
What remained of Hiroshima after the atomic raid. (Imperial War Museum)

Left
Colonel Paul Tibbets Jr (center) and crew of B-29 *Enola Gay*. (US Air Force)

10

GLAMOROUS GLENNIS AND THE X PLANES

The advent of thick-winged fighters capable of speeds around or in excess of 400 mph in level flight and much higher in dives brought to the focus of aerodynamicists, engineers and pilots a deadly force that could literally tear the aircraft apart. This destructive 'enemy' was the air!

Left
Captain Charles 'Chuck' Yeager
in the cockpit of the first X-1
Glamorous Glennis. (Bell
Aerospace Textron)

Below
Bell X-1A under the raised B-29
launch aircraft. (Bell Aerospace
Textron)

Bottom
The first X-1 in powered flight.
(Bell Aerospace Textron)

A known phenomenon, the air flow around such powerful aircraft during fast dives became transonic over the thick wings, forming compressibility shock waves that buffeted the aircraft and could batter the airframe until it broke. Britain first became aware of compressibility problems with the Hawker Tornado prototype of 1939 and then the operational Typhoon, of which many early aircraft were lost with their pilots when the tail assemblies broke off. The thick Clark Y section wing had a lot to do with it, and out of the Typhoon came the Tempest with its thin laminar flow wings. But Britain was not alone, and Lockheed and Republic in America were suffering their own problems with the high-speed P-38 Lightning and P-47 Thunderbolt fighters. Methods of postponing the effect included using thinner and swept wings, as adopted by Messerschmitt during the war years for its Me 262 jet fighter. But, as turbojets made likely the promise of much higher speeds for future Allied aircraft, it became urgent that proper research was started. However, some people believed aircraft would never fly above 650 mph. A catchphrase caught on, 'the sound barrier', representing 761.20 mph at sea level and slowly reducing as the altitude increased.

Under official specification E.24/43, in 1943 design work started in Britain on a supersonic research aircraft. The Miles M-52 was important not only for its research purpose but because it was to achieve supersonic flight using an afterburning turbojet engine. It was estimated that 1,000 mph might be reached at 36,000 feet (660.32 mph representing the speed of sound at that altitude), after a dive from 50,000 feet. However, in 1946 the project was cancelled for two reasons, one economic and the other the mistaken belief that a supersonic aircraft needed swept wings. And the M-52 had straight. Instead, rocket-powered models produced by Vickers were used for research by the Royal Aircraft Establishment, released in mid-air from a Mosquito B. Mk XVI flying off the Scilly Isles.

In America, meanwhile, the engineer Ezra Kotcher had finally achieved a long ambition, to get a manufacturing company to build an aircraft capable of transonic/supersonic research. This appeared in 1945 as the Bell X-1, by then an official secret project. The first of three X-1s began a series of gliding flights in January 1946, later being taken to the remote Air Force research base at Muroc in the Californian desert.

The X-1 encompassed the known and useful features required to undertake supersonic flight, except for having tapering straight wings and not swept. This feature, later, showed the M-52's straight wings would not have been prejudicial to supersonic flight. The X-1's fuselage was bullet shaped, leaving the pilot restricted visibility through the flush glazing. The tiny wings were a mere 3½ inches thick but immensely strong. Indeed, the X-1

had been stressed to +/−18g. Because power came from a four-barrel Reaction Motors rocket motor, which burned the aircraft's fuel at such a rate that under five minutes flight could be managed at full throttle, mid-air launching from beneath a B-29 bomber became essential. One tank each held the liquid oxygen and diluted ethyl alcohol fuel. The last essential for supersonic flight was a pilot with a great deal of nerve!

The 9th day of December 1946 marked the first powered flight of an X-1. After May the program was taken over by NACA and the Air Force, resulting from 6 June 1947 in a new pilot taking the controls from Bell's own test pilot, Chalmers Goodwin. He was Captain Charles 'Chuck' Yeager, the first of the military pilots.

Flight by flight Yeager built upon his previous best speed, until by 10 October 1947 he had managed 99.7 percent of the speed of sound at an altitude of 41,000 feet, known as Mach 0.997. No man living had been so close to breaking the sound barrier. The time had come to edge over into the unknown.

At 10.00 am on the 14th the B-29 lifted off with Yeager in the cabin and the X-1, named *Glamorous Glennis* after his wife, half-submerged in the cutaway bomb-bay. For 20 minutes the bomber made its way to 20,000 feet. Yeager, secretly nursing two broken ribs, walked to a ladder that hung out of the bay and climbed down, then stepped through the X-1's side door and into the cramped but familiar cockpit. It was cold, and the inside of the bay cast a shadow over the X-1's cockpit. He was alone to face whatever dangers lay ahead, a parachute his only means of escape in an emergency once the X-1 was released. He began his flight checks and again when the five minutes warning came over the radio. The cockpit was pressurized and oxygen switched on. Three minutes to release and 'chase' fighters flew into position,

Top Right
Bell X-1A, the first of the second-generation X-1s to explore Mach 2 and high-altitude flight. (Bell Aerospace Textron)

Bottom Right
The swept-wing Bell X-2 was another X-plane for transonic/supersonic research. Two were built, the second making the first powered flight on 18 November 1955. A speed of Mach 3.2 was reached, and an altitude of nearly 126,000 feet. (Bell Aerospace Textron)

Below
The complex Douglas X-3 Stilleto was built to research sustained speeds of up to Mach 3. In consequence it used two Westinghouse turbojet engines married to an extremely slim fuselage and tiny double-wedge wings. Extensive use of titanium was made in its airframe. First flown on 20 October 1952, it only managed transonic speed in level flight. (McDonnell Douglas)

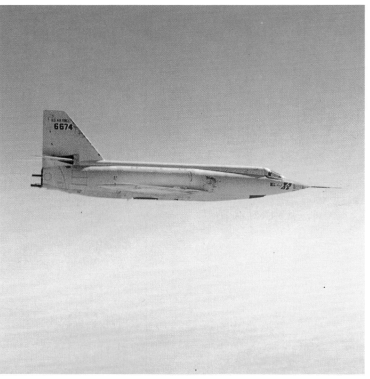

ready to escort Yeager and make visual checks for as long as they could keep up. His heart beat to the reducing seconds. Then, away!

Silently he dropped from the bomber in a high-speed glide, gently pulling back the column to feel control. The aircraft responded. All the time height was being lost and Yeager fired each rocket barrel in turn; the motor had no throttle control as such, the pilot selecting the required power by 'firing' one, two, three or four barrels, each offering 1,500 lb of thrust. He checked the controls. All was well and ready for the real job ahead.

Yeager asked the rocket motor for more power and he recoiled as tremendous acceleration sent the X-1 into climb. At 35,000 feet he reduced power and slowly brought the nose down to level off at 40,000 feet, maintaining a level Mach 0.9+ but now experiencing compressibility buffeting. But for Yeager there was no retreat at this stage. Again power was built up and he pulled back the column, initiating a gentle accelerating climb. Approaching 42,000 feet the Machmeter needle began to shudder with the airframe. Then, suddenly, the buffeting

Below
The X-6 was to be a version of the B-36 bomber with a P-1 nuclear power plant. This photograph shows the Convair NB-36H, a modified B-36 carrying (not powered by) a nuclear reactor in the aft bomb bay to test shielding. No X-6s were built.

Right
Based on the captured German Messerschmitt P.1101, the Bell X-5 investigated the aerodynamic effects of swing-wings. It was first flown on 20 June 1951. This is the second X-5. (Bell Aerospace Textron)

Above
North American X-15, the fastest airplane ever flown. The second X-15 made the first powered flight on 17 September 1959. The X-15 could fly so high, its pilot gained astronaut wings.

Right
The Ryan X-13 Vertijet was built to examine the concept of a vertical take-off and landing jet aircraft. It first flew on 10 December 1955 and made its first full transitions from vertical to horizontal flight and back again on 11 April 1957. (Teledyne Ryan)

Far Right
Another vertical/short take-off and landing concept was the tilting duct, researched from 17 March 1966 by the Bell X-22A. (Bell Aerospace Textron)

stopped and the needle dipped off the dial figures and back again to stop at Mach 1.06 (700 mph). The X-1 flew in the smooth airflow of sonic flight. The sound barrier had been broken for the first time! There was no solid wall of air at Mach 1, only smooth flight beyond. Rocket power was shut down. The X-1 still continued to climb, reaching 45,000 feet before being gently nosed over to begin its 10 minute return to ground. The epic test of man and machine remained secret until late December.

The three Experimental 1s, the X-1s, were only the first of a long line of subsequent X planes built for official research programs. They were immediately followed by derivative aircraft (X-1A, B, etc.) for trials at over twice the speed of sound (Mach 2) and at altitudes of more than 90,000 feet. On 12 December 1953 the X-1A flew at Mach 2.435. It was a larger and improved aircraft but still retained straight wings.

In the late 1980s the X series is still very much alive, with current programs covering the X-31A enhanced fighter maneuverability research aircraft, the X-30 National Aero-Space Plane intended to fly in space at speeds of up to Mach 25 and in the upper atmosphere at Mach 5-15, and the Grumman X-29A forward swept wing technology demonstrator. Between these and the X-1s were piloted and unmanned aircraft for aerodynamic, speed and altitude, swing-wing, airborne nuclear power plant, vertical take-off and space research. A fitting end is to record the Mach 6.72 achieved by the North American X-15 on 3 October 1967, having previously attained 354,200 feet altitude (on 22 August 1963), allowing its pilot to gain astronaut status!

Below
Gaining knowledge used later in the Space Shuttle Orbiter program, the Martin Marietta X-24A was one of several lifting-body research aircraft intended to fly under rocket power and then glide to earth. (Martin Marietta)

Right
One of the current X-plane programs covers the X-29A FSW, intended to explore the benefits of forward swept wings. (Grumman Corporation)

11

RESCUE IN SPACE

On 25 May 1961, when no American astronaut had yet orbited the Earth and the total American flight time in manned suborbital space exploration was 15 minutes and 22 seconds, President John F. Kennedy said in a State of the Union address: 'I believe this nation should commit itself to achieving the goal before this decade is out, of landing a man on the Moon and returning him to Earth. No single space project in this period will be more exciting, or more impressive, or more important for the long-range exploration of space; and none will be so difficult or expensive to accomplish.'

Left
For the first time in the history of
the world, man sets foot on
another planet. (NASA)

Below
Apollo 11 rises clear of the launch
tower at Complex 39A of
Kennedy Space Center. (NASA)

After an expenditure of $24 billion, at 02.56 hours 20 seconds GMT on Monday, 21 July 1969, Neil A. Armstrong stepped from the lunar module *Eagle* and put his foot on the Moon's surface saying, 'That's one small step for a man, one giant leap for mankind.' An estimated 530 million Earth-bound viewers watched the historic event on television. Edwin E. A. Aldrin followed 18 minutes later, while Michael Collins orbited above in the command module *Columbia*. The astronauts tried out the one-sixth gravity in playful manner and then, more seriously, erected the American flag. With no wind to blow it open, a wire frame extended its stars and stripes.

The mission had begun on 16 July and ended with the customary 'splash-down' at 16.49 GMT on the 24th. The total mission time had been 8 days, 3 hours, 18 minutes and 35 seconds, remarkably little more than half an hour longer than had been planned before lift-off.

This mission by Apollo 11 was the culmination of the single-manned Mercury, two-manned Gemini and three-manned Apollo programs. The next Moon landing that year, by Apollo 12, was a mission lasting from 14-24 November, crewed by Charles Conrad, Richard F. Gordon and Alan L. Bean. Five further Moon landings took place, the fourth actual landing by Apollo 15 (a mission of 26 July to 7 August 1971) highlighted by the first use of the lunar roving vehicle, while the Apollo 17 mission of 7-19 December 1972 represented the very last time man set foot on another planet.

But in between Apollo 12 and 14 had come high drama. And yet out of disaster came also triumph and, in true storybook fashion, a rescue in space.

By the time Apollo 13 was launched from Complex 39A at the Kennedy Space Center on 11 April 1970, public interest in Moon landings was already beginning to wane. Both earlier Moon missions had gone well and this was likely to be a repeat performance. It was, however, a heavier spacecraft than those before it, weighing 110,210 lb, the command module *Odyssey* making up just over 12,570 lb of this and the lunar module *Aquarius* about 33,480 lb. To lift such a weight a 6,395,650 lb Saturn V three-stage booster vehicle was adopted, its five first-stage F-1 rocket engines able to produce an initial thrust of over 7½ million pounds, rising to nearly 9 million before cut-off, when stage two would take over.

Apollo 13 had many objectives concerned with geological research of the Moon's surface, among them the deployment of an Apollo Lunar Surface Experiments Package (containing many experiments that included those for measuring the density of neutral particles, lunar heat flow, seismic activity and so on), selenography (mapping and sampling the Moon's surface) in the

Top Left
Emblem of Apollo 8. During 21-27 December 1968 Frank Borman, James Lovell and William Anders became the first men to fly around the Moon. (NASA)

Top Right
Emblem of Apollo 9. During this mission of 3-13 March 1969, the lunar module was carried into space for the first time on a manned mission. It was used to simulate a Moon landing and lift-off. (NASA)

Bottom Left
Apollo 10 was a rehearsal mission for the Moon landing, flown between 18-26 May 1969. Thomas Stafford and Eugene Cernan made two descents to within nine miles of the Moon's surface. (NASA)

Bottom Right
Emblem of the Apollo 12 mission, the second Moon landing. (NASA)

Fra Mauro region, photography of the surface and future areas for exploration and of the Earth, solar wind experiments, communications and television work, and much else beside. Even the spent Saturn V third-stage was to do its bit, intended to impact on the Moon's surface before Apollo 13 landed, the seismographic results measured by an instrument left behind by the crew of Apollo 12 (this was done successfully). On board the spacecraft were also television cameras, allowing many telecasts during the actual flight.

In command of Apollo 13 was James A. Lovell, US Navy, at 42 the oldest of the crew. Two civilians joined him, Fred W. Haise piloting *Aquarius* and John L. Swigert piloting *Odyssey*. Swigert was a last-minute replacement for Thomas Mattingly, who had been in contact with German measles. Right from the start things went wrong. While the second stage of the Saturn V boosted them onwards, one of the five J-2 rocket motors cut out a full 2 minutes 12 seconds early. The four left continued 'burning' for about an extra half-minute beyond the originally scheduled time, but still leaving the spacecraft marginally below expected speed. Once in Earth orbit the S-IVB third stage was again fired, sending the spacecraft into trans-lunar insertion. All was now going well.

Left
Emblem of Apollo 11, the first Moon landing mission. (NASA)

Below
Apollo 11 astronauts: left, Neil A. Armstrong, Michael Collins and Edwin E. Aldrin Jr. (NASA)

Then it happened. Just after a television transmission, at about 55 hours 54 minutes into the flight, the crew heard a loud 'bang'. Swigert reported to Mission Control at Houston at about 21.00 hours local time, 'Hey, we've got a problem here.' An alarm in the connected command/service module indicated a drop in electrical power. A short circuit had ignited wiring insulation in the service module's number 2 oxygen tank, causing it to overheat, explode and rip out the side of the module. Soon after oxygen pressure suddenly went, and the crew saw 'gas' escaping into space. This, in turn, affected two of the three fuel cells which required supplies of oxygen. Now 205,000 miles from Earth and heading unstoppably towards the Moon, the mission was aborted. The over-burdened remaining fuel cell and now-faltering (because of the explosion) other oxygen tank left no choice but to use the lunar module's systems as a 'life raft' in space, and the systems on the command/service module were accordingly run down. Anyway, the command module had only some 15 minutes of power now available! But it appeared to Mission Control that even using the lunar module the crew still had only about 38 hours of oxygen, power and water, and twice that was needed if they were to survive! And the spacecraft had to fly on towards and then around the Moon before it could begin its return flight.

Left
'The Eagle has landed.' Edwin Aldrin climbs down the lunar module *Eagle* to join Neil Armstrong on the Moon's surface. (NASA)

Below
Aldrin takes a lunar soil sample. (NASA)

Above
Apollo 11 experiments deployed included a seismometer and laser reflector. (NASA)

Right
Apollo 13 lift-off on top of the Saturn V launch vehicle. (NASA)

Below
Emblem of Apollo 13, the abandoned third Moon mission. (NASA)

Above
The exhausted Apollo 13 astronauts safe and sound. (NASA)

Right
Apollo 13 recovery on board USS *Iwo Jima* after the 12:07.44 pm splashdown. (NASA)

One hour 35 minutes later the lunar module's Descent Propulsion System was fired to alter the flight path and maneuver the spacecraft into a trajectory that would 'swing' it around the Moon and back towards Earth. As Apollo 13 passed behind the Moon and out of touch with Mission Control everyone waited anxiously for news. All this time thousands of men and women at Mission Control and of the spacecraft's contractors on Earth worked furiously to extend the 'life' of the on-board systems. Techniques for 'powering down' were devised to eke out the life-support systems and bring the crippled 'ship' back to Earth, leaving the crew in discomfort and cold but alive. New maneuvers were calculated, and ground simulators helped develop the necessary procedures to take the spacecraft (in its unexpected shape) safely to re-entry.

It was touch and go. A second Descent Propulsion System 'burn' of 4 minutes 23.4 seconds was performed to reduce the mission time and take the likely landing area from the Indian to the Pacific Ocean. Throughout, the biggest worry was the endurance of the support systems. Even in the lunar module only the Environmental Control System that provided the astronauts with a life-sustaining atmosphere and telemetry radio systems

linking the spacecraft with Mission Control were kept at high power. Further flight maneuvers were made, but the conditions and the tense situation had their toll and twice the crew made mistakes.

The re-entry called for jettisoning of the service module and, 3 hours and 30 minutes later, the lunar module, allowing the command module to continue its flight into Earth's atmosphere. But had the heat shield been damaged? If it had the spacecraft would burn-up on re-entry. Once the service module was released the crew could, at last, see the damage. A large panel had gone and some of the systems were hanging loose. Just prior to releasing the lunar module, the command module was 'powered up' to provide life support.

On 17 April Apollo 13 alighted in the Pacific, only about five miles from the main recovery vessel, the amphibious assault ship USS *Iwo Jima*. The heat shield had been okay! The Accident Review Board found that the number 2 oxygen tank had blown up as a result of its heater switches being welded closed from excessive electrical current and the ensuing eight hours of overheating during ground maintenance. Such a small slip had nearly cost three astronauts their lives.

Above
Astronaut James Irwin saluting the flag during the Apollo 15 mission. The lunar roving vehicle stands by lunar module *Falcon*. The Apennine Mountains near Hadley Delta are seen, by St George's crater. (NASA)

Left
Interior view of Apollo 13 lunar module showing the 'mail box', a hastily contrived arrangement which the astronauts built to use the command module's Lithium canisters to purge carbon dioxide from the lunar module. This arrangement had first been tested on Earth at the Manned Spacecraft Center. (NASA)

INDEX

ACKNOWLEDGEMENTS

There are many individuals, organizations and companies that have contributed to the research, preparation and illustration of this book. Foremost are my colleagues and good friends whose specialist knowledge has added so much to these pages: Maurice Allward, expert on the Wright brothers, David Mondey on the Schneider Trophy races, Kenneth Munson on Lieutenant Commander Richard Byrd, Bill Gunston on Charles Lindbergh and the Hiroshima/Nagasaki attacks, Susan Young and John W. R. Taylor.

Also due for special thanks are Aer Lingus, Aeronautica Macchi (Aermacchi), *The Aeroplane*, US Department of the Air Force, US Department of the Navy, Dornier GmbH, The Goodyear Tire and Rubber Company, Grumman Corporation, Henry Ford Museum, Mitsubishi Heavy Industries, NASA, US National Air and Space Museum (Smithsonian Institution), National Gallery of Ireland, National Library of Ireland, the Royal Air Force Museum at Hendon and Teledyne Ryan.